BAKEWELL

The Ancient Capital of the Peak

TREVOR BRIGHTON

HALSGROVE

First published in Great Britain in 2005

British Library Cataloguing-in-Publication Data
A CIP record for this title is available from the British Library

ISBN 1 84114 419 3

HALSGROVE

Halsgrove House
Lower Moor Way
Tiverton, Devon EX16 6SS
Tel: 01884 243242
Fax: 01884 243325
Email: sales@halsgrove.com
Website: www.halsgrove.com

Frontispiece photograph: *Steps to Church Alley and the old Town Hall. The cells were on the left. Note the gas lamps.* (WATERCOLOUR BY RONALD THORESBY, 1946)

Printed and bound in Great Britain by CPI Bath

CONTENTS

Acknowledgements

Special thanks are due to Michael and Shirley Plant and Pat Brighton who read and checked all the text, weeded out any errors and helped to give the book unity of style. Jane Bradbury and Marian Barker also kept a close eye on the text which they typed onto a word processor. Frank Saunders prepared most of the maps and line drawings, as well as providing photographs, and George Challenger, Stuart Smith and Jan Stetka helped with scanning and the digital photographing of other pictures. Additional photographs were taken by Mavis Mottershaw and Michael Plant.

The following members of the Society also made valuable contributions:

Peter Barker, Gordon Bowring, Barbara Brooke-Taylor, Margaret Cadge, Janet Challenger, Tony Cox, Dorothy Howard, Clifford Mansfield, the late Stephen Penny, Joyce Platts, Vic Pratley, Robert and Kay Robinson, Peter Robinson, Patrick Strange and Elizabeth Wilbur.

The following present and former residents of Bakewell provided photographs and information: the late Roger Baker, Roger Bacon, Herbert Beedham, Michael Cockerton, Peter Coldwell, Ken Croston, Colin Doran, Roy Fox, Dorothy Haythornthwaite, Stephen Kehr, Laurence Knighton, Lord Edward Manners, Kerry Lomas, Audrey and Arthur Monaghan, Steve and Annette Moody, Jack Naylor, David Oulsnam, Graham Pheasey, the late Wolfgang Rudolf, Trevor Smith, Angela Swift, Sid Wardle, John Whibberly, Gerald Worsencroft and Hilary Young.

Thanks are also due to the following organisations for permission to reproduce photographs: the Bakewell Cottage Nursing Home, Derby City Library, Derby City Museums and Art Gallery, *The Derbyshire Times*, the High Peak Hunt, *The Matlock Mercury*, the National Railway Museum, the Peak District National Park Authority and Weston Park Museum, Sheffield.

Generous grants towards the publication of this book were made by the Duke of Devonshire's Trust, the Peak District National Park Authority, Bakewell Town Council and the Derbyshire Dales District Council. For all these contributions the Society offers its sincere thanks.

Introduction

This book has been written, in part, to celebrate the 50th anniversary of the foundation of the Bakewell and District Historical Society in 1954. It also seeks to satisfy a need that long predates the Society, namely for a full historical account of the ancient market town of Bakewell, once capital of the Peak.

The task of writing such a history has been approached on a number of occasions during the past three centuries, but little reached publication. The earliest would-be historian of the town was the late eighteenth-century solicitor and antiquary, James Mander, whose fine residence, Catcliffe House, still stands in King Street. A friend of Dr Samuel Pegge, rector of Whittington, near Chesterfield, and of other notable antiquaries at the end of the eighteenth century, Mander collected books, manuscripts and artefacts which formed the nucleus of Bakewell's first museum. From these sources he began to compile a history which ill-health prevented him from completing, and his collections were scattered.

Some of Mander's material came into the possession of White Watson (1760–1835), the celebrated Bakewell polymath. Born and educated in Sheffield, he joined his uncle, Henry Watson, the marble manufacturer, who lived in the Bath House in Bakewell. Here he established a library and a museum of minerals, fossils and antiquities. No doubt he was instrumental in the attempt by George Nall, the printer and bookseller in the town, to publish by subscription *Bakewell and its Environs* in 1824. This project also came to nought; Nall left for Derby in 1827 having failed to raise subscribers. Watson, always impecunious, could not proceed further, and died in 1835. Many of Watson's papers and books were acquired by William Bateman of nearby Lomberdale Hall. He added to the collections but never published a history. The joint collection of manuscripts and papers accumulated by him and Watson are now pasted into the three volumes entitled *Collections for a History of Derbyshire* in Chatsworth Library.

Of course, short historical accounts of Bakewell appeared in tourist literature of the Peak and in directories and gazetteers from the end of the eighteenth century. In 1884 Edward Andreas Cokayne from Shropshire set up a printing house in the Square in Bakewell. Four years later he issued his *Handbook to Bakewell and its Vicinity*. However, this and other of his publications, such as *A Day in the Peak*, were thin on actual history and broke little new ground.

Cokayne's associate in the newly founded Derbyshire Archaeological and Natural History Society, W.A. Carrington, was a more meticulous scholar and researcher. A native of Bakewell, as archivist to the 8th Duke of Rutland he transcribed the town's manorial records and the household accounts of Haddon Hall which, at the turn of the nineteenth century, were still stored there. Carrington compiled a manuscript history of Bakewell which, sadly, remained unpublished at his death. Particularly useful on the medieval, Tudor and Stuart periods, it is now deposited in the County Record Office at Matlock. It has been corrected and extended by the meticulous research of Anthony Cox, a member of this Society, whose contributions to Chapter 2 have clarified some old misconceptions.

The Bakewell and District Historical Society was fortunate to have as a member the late Dick Allcock, a local schoolmaster who collected old photographs and compiled notes on the town. He published a booklet entitled *Bakewell, an Illustrated History*. This was a collection of brief notes arranged chronologically in periods from Saxon times until the early-twentieth century; it was an encouraging start.

The Society took up the challenge, using its annual *Journal* to publish research on Bakewell as well as to promote occasional publications. In 1984 it published *Source Material for a History of Bakewell*. This was the outcome of a Sheffield University extra-mural class conducted by Trevor Brighton, the Society's Chairman at the time. It next published *Recollections of Bakewell* by Trevor Brighton and Frank Saunders in 1994. This collection of old photographs of the town was principally drawn from Dick Allcock's collections in the Society's museum.

The late Ted Meeke, a former President of the Society, privately printed a compendium of facts and figures entitled *Bakewell in the 19th Century*. Jan Stetka, the Society's present Chairman, had his new research on Bakewell's Anglo-Saxon burh published with the aid of a grant to the Society from Leicester University. Much of his new interpretation of Anglo-Saxon Bakewell constitutes the first chapter of this book.

This history of Bakewell has a number of forebears, therefore, and includes many valuable contributions both from the Society's members and from other residents of the town and district.

Trevor Brighton
President
17 March 2005

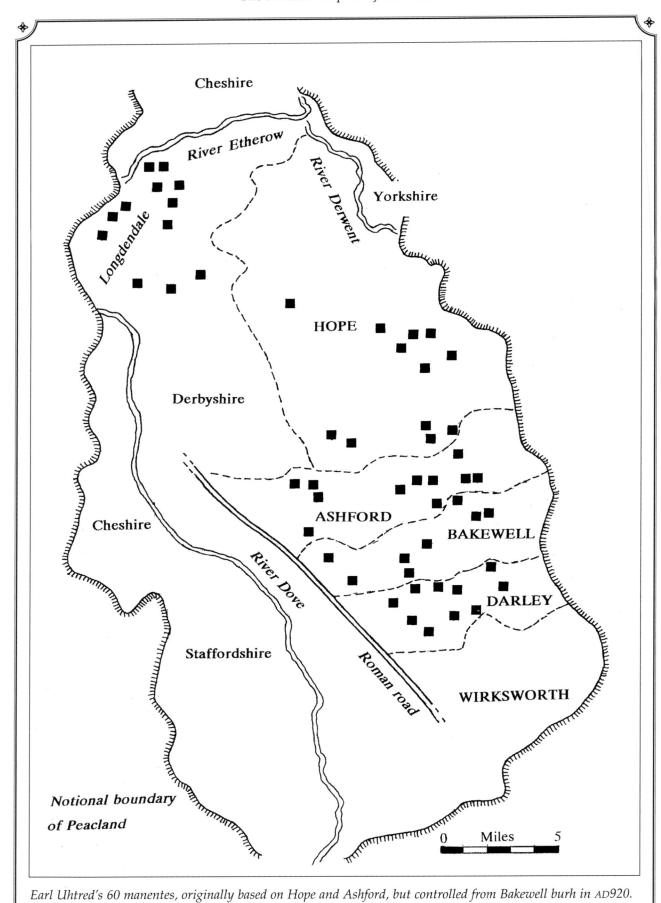

Earl Uhtred's 60 manentes, originally based on Hope and Ashford, but controlled from Bakewell burh in AD920.

✦ CHAPTER 1 ✦

Anglo-Saxon Bakewell

It was events in the Anglo-Saxon period which formed Bakewell as an agricultural market town and shaped the surrounding settlements into the familiar landscape of villages that we see today. The influence of this early period is all around us. The vast majority of local names are Anglo-Saxon, and much of our local land disposition has its origins in this period, for example the name of the Peak District itself, the parish of Bakewell and the county of Derbyshire. In addition, Bakewell church has probably the largest collection of fragments of free-standing Anglo-Saxon sculpture in the land, the Peak District generally being rich in Anglo-Saxon grave goods.

The period consists of a succession of conquests by the Angles in the seventh century, the Vikings in the ninth, the Saxons in the tenth and the Normans (Northmen or French Vikings) in the eleventh. Each conquest tended to destroy the written records of the previous one, so there are few local contemporary documents on which to base a history. Nor do we have the help of a contemporary historian for Mercia (the Midlands), as in the case of Bede for Northumbria or Asser for the Saxon lands.

Of the Germanic tribes who sailed across the North Sea in search of new lands in England it was the Angles who first came to the Peak and who named it thus. Coming from the north Netherlands (Friesland) and adjacent areas of north Germany, they sailed into the Humber and up the Trent, where they settled to form Mercia, 'the borderlands'. Archaeological evidence from their earliest graves suggests settlement in the sixth century. Some gradually occupied lands to the north, along the River Derwent to Northworthy (the northern enclosure), their name for Derby, and further north still they noticed a significant change in the terrain by the time they reached Wirksworth (Wyre's enclosure). These newcomers had left the valleys of the Trent and the Derwent and were entering a land of limestone crags and gritstone tors which they called Peacland, the pointy land. In so doing they became the first 'Peacsaetan', Peak dwellers.

There is no evidence of Roman settlement in the Bakewell area, so when the newcomers arrived the local Celts would have been living in family farmsteads much as they had done for the previous thousand years of the Iron Age. The Angles became the new overlords and their contribution to farming can be deduced from the prevalence of place names ending in 'ley', meaning woodland clearing. Along the Derwent from Matlock we have Dar*ley* Dale, with Wens*ley* to the west and Far*ley* to the east. Then Rows*ley*, Bee*ley*, Lang*ley*, near present-day Chatsworth, and Pils*ley*. These seven settlements have Anglian names, denoting woodland clearance along a length of the river Derwent of about seven miles, and there are others ending in the plural 'lees'. Derwent, meaning 'abounding with oaks', is probably the only surviving Celtic name in the Bakewell area.

Cameron, in his *Place Names of Derbyshire*, states that the stems of these 'ley' names are typical seventh-century Anglian names. Thus we have a picture of the incoming Angles, probably with a superior fighting and farming technology, organising the clearance of woodland down into the river valleys so as to extend the area which could be farmed. Anglian burial barrows, of which 40 have been found to date in Peacland, date this activity to the seventh century.

At the time of their arrival here the Angles were pagan, as is shown by their local place names Wensley (the grove or clearing dedicated to Woden) and Friden (the dene or valley dedicated to the goddess Frig). However, Christianity came to Mercia in the mid-seventh century and it is likely to have penetrated to the Bakewell area fairly soon afterwards. Grave goods found in two Anglian burials near Bakewell are evidence of this. In the first, the finds included a helmet ornamented with both a Christian cross on the nose piece and a boar – a warrior's symbol of Woden – on the crest. The second is at White Low, near Winster where, though the manner of burial was pagan, gold jewellery with Christian emblems was buried with its owner in her barrow grave. Our word 'low' is derived from the Anglian 'hlaw', meaning mound, burial barrow or hill.

From the numerous ingots that have been found stamped with Roman inscriptions it is well known that the Romans mined lead in Peacland. It seems that lead mining continued when the Romans left and may have been the major attraction for the Mercians in occupying this area, particularly as silver occurs geologically with lead. Perhaps for this reason Anglo-Saxon royal interest in the area always seems to have been strong, although Peacland is on marginal agricultural land well to the north of the main centres of the Mercian kingdom. The Domesday Book in 1086 records all the mines, including one at Bakewell, as being on royal land, so

Left: *Remains of a warrior's helmet with a cross on the nasal. From a seventh-century burial at Benty Grange, seven miles south-west of Bakewell.* (SHEFFIELD CITY MUSEUM)

Right: *Reconstruction of the Benty Grange helmet.*

Left: *Gold filigree cross set with a central garnet. From a seventh-century burial mound at White Low, on Winster Moor, seven miles south of Bakewell.* (SHEFFIELD CITY MUSEUM)

Right: *Disc pendant of the same date and from the same mound.*

it is probable that from early in the Anglian occupation Bakewell was a royal estate with lead mining around Lathkill Dale, with smelting nearby and with the distribution of the metal controlled by the Mercian rulers. Because of royal power it would have been at least nominally Christian and would probably have had a church.

Ninth Century:
The Coming of the Vikings

Since the late-eighth century Norse and Danish Vikings had raided the coast of England, but serious conquest began only with the coming of the Great Army of the Danes in AD865. In 873 they overwintered in Repton and by 877 had begun their settlement of north-east Mercia, including Peacland. Northworthy became a major Viking fortified place, now with its new name of Derby. A lack of distinctive pagan and Danish artefacts suggests, however, that the newcomers quickly adopted both Christianity and the local culture.

Peacland was now under the Danelaw and was 'ruled' by the Danish army at Derby. The Danish armies divided their territories into 'wapentakes', a term which means literally 'the flourishing of spears' and may refer to the practice whereby the 12 most prominent Danish landholders would meet and signify their acceptance of a resolution by waving their spears in the air; they were ready to defend that resolution by the use of those spears if necessary.

Bakewell was in the vanished wapentake of Hamenstan, stretching from Glossop in the north to Ashbourne in the south, an area largely lacking place-name evidence of Danish settlement. Around Bakewell, indeed, there are only two Danish place names, Flagg and Rowland (Domesday Book 'Flagun' and 'Ralunt'). Since these are upland places on the margin of cultivation, this tends to suggest that the main centres of cultivation of the Anglian Pecsaetan were not settled by the invading Danes; the Pecsaetan presumably paid their dues to the Danish army rather than to Mercia. In contrast, over the moors to the east of Bakewell the wapentake of Scarsdale, centred on today's Chesterfield, was well settled by the Danish Vikings and is dense with Danish place names.

By 900 King Alfred had retaken the Saxon lands in

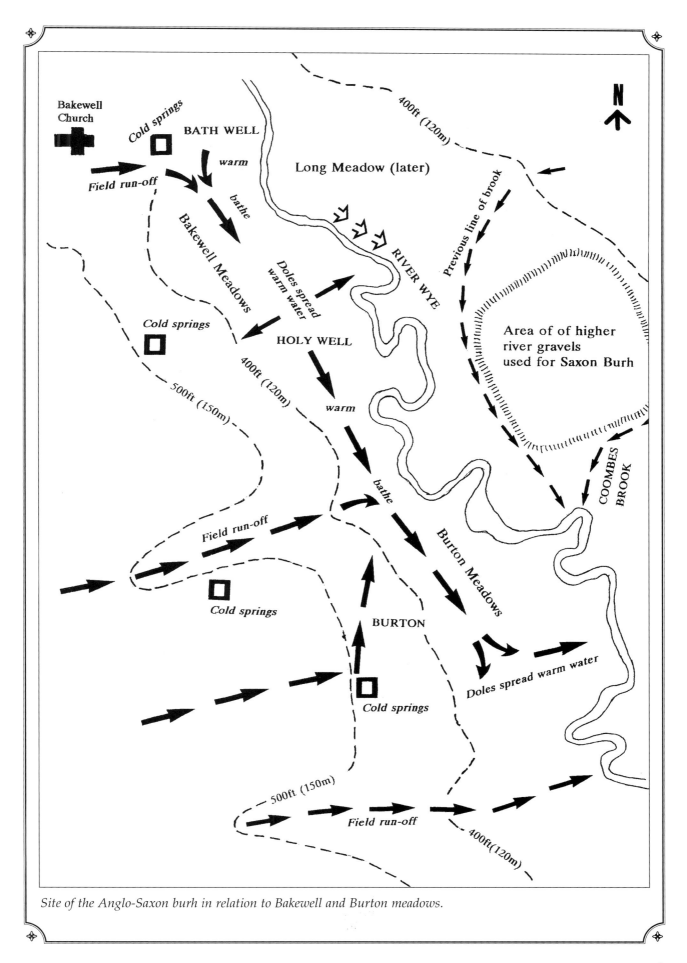

Site of the Anglo-Saxon burh in relation to Bakewell and Burton meadows.

The Bakewell Cross. Shaft (c.920) with head missing. (ENGRAVING BY J.H. LeKEUX (1812–96))

Early photograph (c.1900) of the gritstone shaft, showing vine scroll decoration.

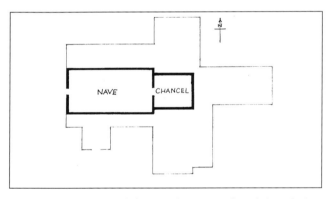

A suggested layout of the Anglo-Saxon church in relation to that of the existing church. The chancel and a possible crypt beneath were on the site of the later tower.

the south from the Vikings and had been succeeded by his son, Edward, King of Wessex, respected as the over-king of all the Saxon lands and of what remained of Anglian Mercia. It was he who called on Uhtred, the younger son of the English Earl of Northumbria, to buy part of Peacland from the Vikings, probably in order to extend English influence. A land charter of about 906 contains the following: 'to Uhtred, 60 manentes of land at Hope and Ashford, the estate he had bought from the Danes by order of King Edward for 20 pounds of gold and silver.'

This is the first example in England of land being purchased rather than being granted by the king, and Uhtred seems to have bought all of the northern part of Hamenstan wapentake, from Glossop in the north as far south as Darley, and including Bakewell. Hope and Ashford, mentioned in the charter, were probably the principal settlements in northern Peacland at that time as the principal trackway in the region, the Portway, passed through them. Bakewell was bypassed and was therefore of less importance.

The Anglo-Saxon Chronicles from 911 to 920 are a story of the re-conquest from the Danes of the land from the Thames to the Humber. This was achieved by King Edward's Saxon forces in the east in concert with those of his sister, Ethelflæd, Lady of the Mercians, in the west, and culminated in Bakewell in 920. Ethelflæd's army re-took Derby from the Danes in 917 and those at Nottingham surrendered to King Edward in 918.

Vital to this re-conquest was the systematic construction of a network of strongholds called burhs. A burh is an embanked enclosure designed to act as a base for Saxon warriors and a safe haven for the local Anglo-Saxon population and they were located so that people could reach one within a day's journey of 20 miles. King Alfred built 30 burhs, King Edward 20 and Ethelflæd ten. Having constructed burhs by the River Mersey and at Manchester in 919 to counter a threat from that quarter, Edward now needed to plug the gap between Manchester and Derby with a final burh in Peacland. The Anglo-Saxon Chronicle for 920 reads:

… he then went to Badecan Wiellon [Bakewell] *in*

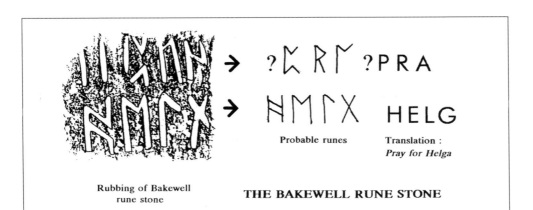

→ ?ᚲ ᚱᚠ ?PRA

→ ᚺᛖᛚᚷ HELG

Probable runes

Translation :
Pray for Helga

**Rubbing of Bakewell
rune stone**

THE BAKEWELL RUNE STONE

The Bakewell Rune Stone.   (SHEFFIELD CITY MUSEUM)

Peacland and ordered a burh to be made in the neighbourhood and manned. Then the King of the Scots and the whole Scottish nation accepted him as father and lord; so also did Ragnald [the Norse ruler in York] and the sons of Eadwulf [including Uhtred] and all those who live in Northumbria, English and Danish, Norsemen and others.

Unfortunately the Chronicle does not specify where the northern rulers 'accepted him'. Was it in Bakewell, was it on the Northumbrian border or was it by remote agreement?

A document of King Edward's time, now known as the 'Burghal Hidage', tells us how big the Bakewell burh would have been. Listing 33 burhs, together with the number of hides (family farms) assigned to each, it has a final section which specifies that every hide should be represented by one man who will be required to build and defend about four feet of wall. We know from other sources that the number of hides in Peacland was 1,200, so applying the formula to the Bakewell burh gives us a length of wall bank of 1,200 x 4 feet, making 4,800 feet, or a little under a mile.

The probable site of Bakewell burh is about one mile south-west of Bakewell church. It is on a terrace of river gravels bounded by streams on two of its sides with the remains of an embankment on the other two. With each side a quarter of a mile long, the corners are rounded so that the total perimeter is a little under a mile. It is on the opposite side of the River Wye to Burton meadows and the site of the lost medieval village of Burton, listed in the Domesday Book as an outlying farm to Bakewell manor and whose name is derived from burh-tun, meaning 'the farm near to, or supporting, the burh'.

In 926 Athelstan, Edward's son and successor, confirmed to Uhtred the land which he had bought 20 years earlier. This is recorded in a charter which reads:

Athelstan, King of the Anglo-Saxons, to Uhtred, for 300 mancuses of gold, 60 manentes of land at Hope and

Ashford [probably including Bakewell], the estate he had bought from the Danes by order of King Edward for 20 pounds of gold and silver.

By this time, with the choice of site for the burh and the development of agriculture in the area, Bakewell, having become the principal settlement in Peacland, Athelstan passed laws to safeguard property and trade in such Saxon towns. Uhtred, who may be considered the founder of Bakewell town, was termed a 'soldier and leader' and was a frequent visitor to the court of King Athelstan, where his name appears in the lists of witnesses to charters. By 930 he was termed Ealderman (Earl) with the sense 'Governor', which probably means that he was the governor of all Northern Mercia. His last charter, of 949, reads:

Eadred, King of the English, ruler of the Northumbrians, emperor of the heathen [Vikings] and protector of the Britons, to Governor Uhtred land at Badecanwelle [Bakewell] free of all but the three common dues.

There is mention of a 'coenubium' at Bakewell. This is a monastery and 'minster', or mother church for the area. The form of the charter suggests the king is removing all taxes and rental burdens from the land in order that the proceeds may be devoted without encumbrance to the service of the church. The minster is thus being endowed, though those working the land are still responsible for the three common dues – army service and work on bridges and fortifications.

It is at today's Bakewell church that we have the most tangible remains from Uhtred's time. The great cross shaft in the churchyard is thought to have been taken there in about 1600 from the Hassop crossroads, one and a half miles to the north. The scenes carved on its western face are Christian, those on its eastern face pagan. It may be that the Christian story which appears on the side facing the church was taught through the pagan mythology which

Anglian cross shaft (c.1000) in churchyard. Brought from Beeley Moor.

appeared on the other side, facing the countryside where many of the people were still pagan.

In the south porch of the church are many fragments of Anglo-Saxon wayside crosses which were discovered in the foundations of the Early English church tower when it was rebuilt in 1841. They are in a variety of styles – Mercian, Anglo-Danish, Northumbrian and Norse – the result, no doubt, of the ethnic mix in Peacland at the time when King Edward was accepted as 'father and lord'. Some of the more interesting pieces, now in Sheffield Museum, include a fragment of a stone carved with a runic inscription, probably Bakewell's first written record. Runes, used widely across Europe before the Latin alphabet was taught by monks with the coming of Christianity, are characters formed by straight lines suitable for carving in wood, bone or stone. The Bakewell rune stone has missing characters to the right but appears to say 'Pray for Helga'.

Uhtred's Bakewell also saw the establishment of the common field system of village agriculture, under which villagers worked strips of arable land scattered throughout the common fields and had grazing rights in the meadow and pasture land. This served the community throughout the Middle Ages and lasted, in an attenuated form, until the enclosure of the open fields at the beginning of the nineteenth century; traces of it can clearly be seen even now. Installed in northern Mercia in general in the tenth century, this system brought family farms together into vills and gave Peacland the landscape of villages that is so familiar today.

Bakewell had four common fields, and its geographical position, with its valley of water meadows, its sheltered western shelf for plough land and ample moorland on the limestone plateau for pasture, made it eminently suitable for this farming system. In a common field system a critical resource is the amount of meadow on which to produce hay for the oxen to eat during winter, which in turn determines how many fields can be ploughed and hence how many people can be fed. Bakewell was fortunate not only in the quantity of water-meadow but also in its quality.

Bakewell's meadowland stretched from the present town centre to Holywell, in the recreation-ground, a little way down the present A6, and was flooded each spring, thus fertilising it with calcium from limestone springs and with leachings from the arable fields and farmyards. Of particular value to Bakewell was the fact that a significant volume of the spring water was naturally warm. This meant that the grass of these meadows began to grow much earlier than would otherwise have been the case, enabling more hay to be grown during the season so that more oxen could be sustained during the winter months. The warm springs were thus a valuable resource in a medieval economy, so it was small wonder that one of them was honoured with the title 'holy'. Meadowland was divided into strips called doles, which were reallocated each season. Although all vestiges of these have disappeared from Bakewell, along with the warm springs, which were ducted underground early in the nineteenth century, those of the settlement of Burton are, at the time of writing, clearly visible on the outskirts of Bakewell, a short distance down the A6.

The importance of the warm springs appears to be reflected in Bakewell's name. In its earliest form, in the Anglo-Saxon Chronicle of 920, it is 'Badecan Wiellon' or Badeca's springs. Cameron's *Place Names of Derbyshire* confirms that Badeca is a man's name of the seventh-century type. However, glossaries of Anglo-Saxon names do not record any other occurrences of this name so Badeca was probably named after the place where he lived, its most significant feature being the warm springs. Another reference to 'Badecan' appears in the Burghal Hidage, where the name is attached to Bath, Somerset, thus seeming to confirm its association with warm springs. By the end of the Saxon era, therefore, warm springs had given Bakewell both its name and its position of prominence in the area.

✦ CHAPTER 2 ✦

A Medieval Parish, Manor and Market Town

Whether or not the Peak settlers put up any resistance to the mounted detachments of the Conqueror's army in 1066 is not known. Certainly the clerks and officials who came hard on the army's heels recorded prosperous manors along the Rivers Wye and Derwent in the Domesday Book of 1086. Their locations amid underwood and scrub, where deer and boar abounded, appealed to the Norman passion for hunting. It was not surprising, then, that William I took the best pickings from the manors that had belonged to Edward the Confessor and his successor, Harold. Bakewell was the prize of the Peak and the first description we have of the town appears as follows in the Domesday Book:

In Badequella [Bakewell] *with 8 outliers, King Edward* [the Confessor] *had 18 carucates* [ploughlands] *of taxable land. Land for 18 ploughs. The King* [William] *now has in lordship 7 ploughs; 33 villagers and 9 small holders; 2 priests and a church and under them 2 villagers and 5 smallholders who have 11 ploughs altogether. 1 man at arms has 16 acres of land and 2 smallholders. This is a mill worth 10s.8d.* [53p]; *a lead mine; 80 acres of meadow and underwood 1 league long and 1 wide. Of this land 3 carucates belong to the church. Henry de Ferrers claims one carucate in Haddon. The outliers of this manor are* [Nether] *Haddon, Holme, Rowsley, Burton, Conkesbury, One Ash, Monyash,* [Over] *Haddon.*

Bakewell was the wealthiest manor in the Peak and, outside the borough of Derby, its church equalled Repton's in supporting two priests. It was not in a strong position militarily and the old burh had ceased to function a century and a half earlier. Peak's Arse (Castleton), where the Norman William Peveril I built a wooden castle, had military pre-eminence in the Peak. Bakewell grew as a cluster of small farms and cottages on the western slopes of the Wye and in 1086 had a population of between 200 and 300. Its Anglo-Saxon church still lay at its western edge but no defences around the town have been discovered and the belief of some that a second Anglo-Saxon burh was the basis of the town's development is difficult to prove. The fact that the Portway, an ancient route from Derby, passes by the town to the northwest has also led to the suggestion that the important market that grew up had its origins near to the Portway rather than below the church near to the river, where it was certainly located by the late Middle Ages.

As farming and lead-mining developed and the

Domesday Book entry in Latin for Bakewell, 1086.

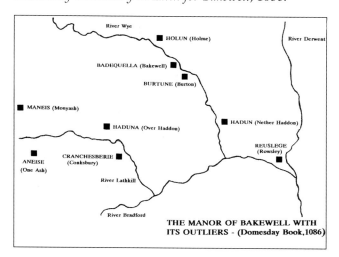

Map of the Manor of Bakewell with its outliers as described in the Domesday Book, 1086.

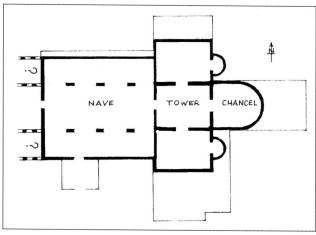

A suggested plan of the Norman church in relation to the present church. The western towers are indicated, though they may not have existed.

The earthed up Norman west door of the church.
(ENGRAVING BY J. STORER AFTER A DRAWING BY H. MOORE, 1830)

The Norman west door of the church, in its present decayed state.

The remains of an intended staircase to the north-western Norman tower, discovered in a 1902 excavation and removed to the west boundary of the churchyard.

The interior of the nave before remodelling in 1852.
(WATERCOLOUR (C.1835) BY J.L. PETIT)

town's population and prosperity grew, so its church flourished. Between 1100 and 1108 King Henry I granted Bakewell and its outlier, Haddon, along with other Peakland manors, to William Peveril (or Peverel) I, making him the wealthiest landowner in the Peak. It was probably he who took down Bakewell's Anglo-Saxon church, erecting on the same sloping site a stronger, more imposing structure using shale from the opposite side of the river, where the beds of this material are nearer to sandstone than gritstone.

Originally the new church was conceived with two western towers either side of a west door, a nave, two short transepts with apses (semicircular chapels) to the east, an apsidal chancel and a low, capped tower over the crossing. It was planned like Derbyshire's only surviving three-towered Norman church, of St Michael and St Mary at Melbourne. However, Bakewell's two western towers appear not to have been completed and today their walled-up entrance arches are still visible, inside the church, at the west end of the north and south nave aisles. The two western Norman bays, which still stand, give us some idea of the severe solidity of the work. The arches are plain and unmoulded with some weak billet motifs as the only decoration. Outside survives the chevron moulding on traces of the blind, interlaced arcading of the west front. Below this is the west door, once the decorative jewel which

The remaining Norman work still visible at the north-west end of the nave.

welcomed Peak dwellers into the new church, though the signs of the zodiac and accompanying pattern work, still decipherable in the late-eighteenth century, are decayed beyond recognition. The lovely tower doorway of nearby Bradbourne church gives us some idea of how it once looked before the friable stone mouldered away.

Troubled Times under Stephen and the Angevin Kings

The new church was probably finished by 1135, the year in which Henry I died without a surviving male heir. Norman peace and stability were shattered when his daughter, Matilda, tried to secure the Crown, only to see it seized by her cousin Stephen. In the debilitating conflict which followed, powerful barons took and changed sides for their own gain. One such was William Peveril II, lord of the 'Honour of the Peak', which included Bakewell. He threw in his lot with Stephen and took his feudal Peakland tenants into battle. How many Bakewellians fought with Peveril for Stephen is not known, but at the battle of Lincoln in 1141 he and his king were captured by Matilda's forces and his estates were confiscated. To secure his loyalty these were restored to him in 1143, but Matilda's husband, Geoffrey Plantagenet, Count of Anjou, did not trust him and was preparing to grant Peveril's lands to Ranulf II, Earl of Chester. However, in 1153 the earl

was poisoned, allegedly by Peveril himself, and in the following year Henry II, on his accession, immediately re-confiscated Peveril's estates. These were distributed to various royal supporters, though the Crown retained Castleton and its fortress and much of the old 'Honour of the Peak', including Bakewell.

So Bakewell passed, on Henry II's death, to his first son, Richard I, and then to his second, John. They disposed of the royal holdings in Bakewell, which passed forever from the direct control of the Crown. First, in 1192, the land endowments and the tithes of the rebuilt church were granted by Prince John, Count of Mortain, in his brother Richard's absence abroad, to his friend and counsellor, Hugh de Nonant, Bishop of Coventry and Lichfield, and to the Dean and Chapter of that see. From that day to this the Dean and Chapter of Lichfield have held the advowson of Bakewell, that is, the right to appoint the vicar.

The possession of the tithes of Bakewell parish was a matter of contention, leading to active hostility between the Dean and Chapter of Lichfield and Lenton Priory, near Nottingham. The latter, a satellite house of the great monastery of Cluny in Burgundy, was founded by William Peveril, who endowed it with part of the tithes of Holme and Bakewell, Peveril's sub-tenant, William Avenel, granting the tithes from Haddon. Lichfield challenged Lenton's claim, asserting the grant made by Prince John and confirmed by him after his accession as king in 1199. Following persistent disputes the matter was referred to the Pope for judgement. His representatives in England arrived at a compromise whereby Lenton collected the tithes but the Dean and Chapter received a payment from the Priory. However, this does not appear to have been acceptable to Lenton, which presumably withheld the payment. Then, in 1279, according to the Calendar of Inquisitions, the Dean and Chapter's patience ran out:

Master William de Wymundisham and Master Simon de Balidene, by consent of the dean of Lichfield, came to Bachequelle [Bakewell] in the Peak accompanied by many armed persons, and Master Simon… approached Haddun [Haddon] and took corn of the prior of Lenton from his house and caused tithes, whereof the prior had been in possession since the foundation of his house [i.e. priory], to be collected from the fields of Haddun. The said Master William and certain armed persons approached the fields of Hulm [Holme] and Bachequelle and likewise took corn and tithes.

The Prior of Lenton protested to King Henry III, who summoned both parties to his court at Winchester in 1279. He reasserted the earlier papal judgement but increased the annual payment of Lenton Priory to 40 marks (£26.66p). Presumably this arrangement held until Henry VIII's Dissolution of the priory, when the

Bakewell's timber fortress as it might have appeared on Castle Hill in the twelfth century.

(DRAWING BY FRANK SAUNDERS)

The overgrown remains of the man-made motte, or mound, on Castle Hill. The wooden Norman keep stood here, not the Saxon burh.

The Norman gate tower at Haddon Hall.

(LITHOGRAPH BY SAMUEL RAYNER, 1836)

View into the chapel at Haddon Hall, c.1890. The font is Norman and the lancet windows Early English.

tithes would have reverted to Lichfield.

Next, after his accession in 1189, King Richard himself disposed of the royal manor of Bakewell to a loyal Essex landowner, Ralph Gernon. Ralph seems to have built the first manor-house in Bakewell, above the town to the south-west of the church. No physical trace of it survives, though its name is preserved in the housing estate known as Moorhall.

It may also have been Ralph who, in about 1190, built Bakewell's castle. This was erected on a man-made motte, or mound, overlooking the ford in the river from its eastern bank. Presumably it served to guard the entrance to the dale villages and to the central market town, Bakewell itself. Today the overgrown site, which offers the public fine views across the valley, has nothing structural remaining above the ground, though the earthworks of the castle's motte and bailey can still be seen. Excavations conducted by Manchester University in 1976 finally exploded the old eighteenth-century belief that here was the original site of Edward the Elder's burh of 920. Instead, the limited discoveries of artefacts, including sherds of pottery, indicated that the stronghold was constructed of timber and was typical of numerous small fortifications that sprang up in the troubled times of the twelfth century. Such wooden structures soon decayed.

Meanwhile, a mile and a half downstream from Bakewell castle, another and more substantial fortified house was being built of stone at Nether Haddon. Since William Peveril had been dispossessed of his Peak manors in 1153, the lord of Nether and Over Haddon was now William Avenel. It was he who built a hall, a small chapel and a cluster of service buildings, linked by a curtain wall, at Nether Haddon. Vestiges of these buildings are still visible at Haddon Hall.

William Avenel II had no male heir, so the Haddon estates were divided between his two sons-in-law. Simon Basset acquired half the property, including a house in Over Haddon; Richard de Vernon, who had married Avenel's elder daughter, was granted the other half, with the newly built hall and chapel and with adjoining orchards at Nether Haddon. Gradually, during the next century or so, the Bassets released their holdings to the Vernons, whose wealth and influence burgeoned following advantageous marriages and a lucrative income from the local lead mines. The family was established at Haddon Hall for the next 400 years.

The Expansion of the Parish and the Rebuilding of the Church

The wealthy landowners, knights, merchants and priests who lived in the large parish of Bakewell in the twelfth and thirteenth centuries usually found their last repose within the church of All Saints. Excavations for the foundations of a new tower in 1840 laid bare their sarcophagi and the decorated grave slabs that covered them. The latter are now arranged in the south porch, forming one of the finest collections of their type in England. All bear a decorative cross, carved in various patterns in low relief – but, as is generally the case, none carries any name or inscription. One can only guess at the occupation and status of those interred from the symbols carved or incised beside their cross. Thus, shears may denote a wool merchant, a sword a knight, a bow and arrow an archer, a bugle horn a forest warden and a chalice a priest.

People like these made benefactions of land or money which enabled the church to be altered and partially rebuilt in the new style of the pointed arch known as 'Early English'. First, about 1230, the south

Twelfth- and thirteenth-century gritstone sarcophagi excavated during the early-Victorian restoration of the church. The porch is fifteenth century. The sundial was carved by White Watson in 1799, originally for the south wall of the Newark.

Part of the fine collection of twelfth- and thirteenth-century tomb slabs in the church porch.

Sheep shears, indicating the grave of a wool merchant.

transept was replaced by the 'new work' (or Newark) – an elongated arm with elegant lancet windows and a beautiful south door. The Norman central tower was taken down and on its inadequate foundations a low 'Early English' tower and lead cap were erected on four finely moulded, pointed arches.

Slightly later in the thirteenth century a new north nave aisle was pushed out level with the north transept and Gothic entrances were opened into the north and south aisles of the nave. The three apsidal chapels were removed from the two transepts and the chancel, the last being extended and squared off behind the high altar. More light was admitted by inserting simple Gothic windows with Y-tracery in the nave aisles and the chancel. Of the early-twelfth-century Norman church only the nave arcades, the blocked off western nave arches and the west front with its fine door remained. The extended chancel was furnished, as befitted a wealthy church, with a high altar approached by steps, stepped sedilia (seats for priests and acolytes assisting at Mass), a double piscina (a stone basin and drain for washing the chalice), an aumbry (a cupboard for reserving the sacrament) and stalls for the priests.

Yet, despite all this fine show and the fact that the church of All Saints was the third most valuable parish living in England, the Dean and Chapter of Lichfield siphoned off most of its income. In 1280 the vicar, who had to support in turn two assistant priests, a deacon and a sub-deacon, was paid 20 marks a year (£13.33p), until the Archbishop of Canterbury intervened and had the stipend increased by 10 marks.

The clergy moved around the large parish helping to establish chapels of ease and often saying Mass until assistant priests could be afforded. The following chapelries within the parish were expected to contribute towards maintaining the fabric of the mother church and the upkeep of the churchyard:

Ashford	Baslow	Beeley	Buxton	Chelmorton
Hassop	Longstone	Monyash	Over Haddon	
Rowland	Rowsley	Sheldon	Taddington	

As the years passed and these villages increased in population, so they pressed the Dean and Chapter to allow their chaplains rights of baptism, matrimony and burial. These concessions would reduce their attachment and obligation to the mother church which in turn feared an accompanying decline in its income. A parochial struggle lay ahead.

The Gernons

For nine generations, a period of almost 200 years, the manor of Bakewell remained in the possession of the Gernons, a family whose ancestor, Robert, may have fought with William the Conqueror and who had been rewarded with 31 lordships in Essex.

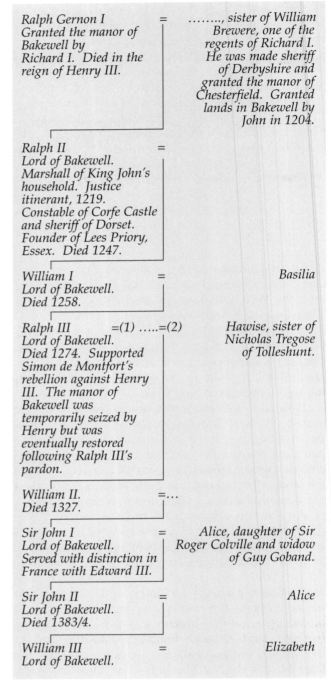

In the recently erected Newark, Ralph Gernon III created a chantry chapel and dedicated it to the Virgin Mary. To maintain a priest there to celebrate Mass daily for the salvation of his soul he bequeathed land and a house to the south-east of the churchyard, where now stands the old Town Hall. The house became a guildhall for members of the Guild of Our Lady, as well as a lodging for the chantry priest. Guilds also included lesser folk who paid a priest for saying an occasional Mass for their collective souls. The chantry priest was often excused parochial duties, though sometimes bequests provided for him to teach boys in the parish, thus creating the roots of many of the ancient grammar schools.

Bakewell bridge c.1900, originally built c.1300.

Sketch of Bakewell bridge by John Byng, later Viscount Torrington, 1789. This is the earliest known illustration of the bridge before it was widened on the up-stream side in 1828. Note the plinth for a lamp or a religious shrine.

To the Gernons can be attributed the chantry of Our Lady, the vanished castle, the fine stone bridge over the Wye, which supplanted the ford in about 1300, and the manor-house of Moor Hall, occupied by their steward. The present home for the elderly, Gernon Manor, has no association with the Gernons. The family appears to have resided at the heart of its landed holdings in Essex and its members were interred there, not in Bakewell.

However, this does not imply neglect of the manor of Bakewell and in the 200 years or so of their tenure from the Crown, the Gernons may be said to have maintained law and order in their manorial courts. Through these they governed the economy of the land, the social order in the town and the conduct of markets and fairs, as laid down by royal charter.

As was usual in England, there were two manorial courts, presided over by the steward in the lord's absence. The first was the court leet, which was a court of record granted by prescription or charter by the king to meet annually or semi-annually. Of Anglo-Saxon origin, it had powers of arrest within the confines of the manor and the presentation of offenders before it. Freemen, that is those having freehold land without feudal ties to the lord of Bakewell, were exempt from its jurisdiction by the later Middle Ages. The unfree, villeins and serfs, were not exempt. Capital crimes and such serious offences as grievous bodily harm, affray, robbery and so on were dealt with in the Assize courts at Derby or Nottingham.

Secondly, the court baron was a civil court called by the lord to deal with the customs of the manor, maintain the duties and services owed by the tenants and impose penalties in the form of amercements, or fines. A jury constituted from the freeholders of Bakewell adjudicated on the cases brought before it. By the end of the Middle Ages the distinctions between the courts leet and baron had become blurred and thereafter they were merged.

The records of these early courts have not survived but from the late-sixteenth century hundreds of examples exist to show the courts in action, especially in regulating the working of the land and the rights governing the use of the commons, meadows and pastures.

By the Norman period Bakewell was operating a common three-field system such as was usual in the Midlands and much of the rest of England, but not in the Peak. Some of the villages within the parish of Bakewell on the poorer upland soils worked two or even one field. Outside the three fields and also used in common were meadow, pasture and common land. The arable fields were rotated for the cultivation of oats, wheat, barley, beans and peas. During the fallow period, when one field was rested, animals were allowed to graze and manure the ground for strictly specified periods governed by the manorial courts. Fines were imposed on those who did not tend or adequately demarcate their crops within the strips of land allocated to them; lead miners were punished for walking through the crops as a short-cut to the mines and sheep and cattle which were allowed to stray were removed by the pinder and impounded in the pinfold. At the time of writing, Pinfold Cottage on Monyash Road indicates the old cattle pound and behind it, amid later drystone walls, can plainly be seen the old ridge and furrow, marks of the medieval common field system which persisted until final enclosure in 1810.

Whilst protecting the rural economy, the manorial courts also regulated the markets and fairs held in the town. These enabled the sale of produce and live-stock not only from the town but from the far-flung parish and beyond. They also provided the lord with a lucrative income in fees and tolls.

The date of Bakewell's first royal charter granting its lord a market is unknown. We do know that Henry II had granted a fair to the town on 29 February 1254 by which Sir William Gernon I was allowed an annual fair lasting 15 days from the Feast of Saints Philip and James. However, in the pleas of Quo Warranto (by what warrant) held at Derby in 1381/2, John Gernon II claimed the right

Ridge and furrow fields near Monyash Road. These are among the clearest vestiges of the medieval fields still visible around the town.

to hold a market in Bakewell every Monday and a fair lasting three days each year at the Vigil and following the Feast of the Assumption of the Virgin on 13–15 August. He maintained that this right to a market and a fair had been enjoyed by him, his ancestors and all previous lords of Bakewell since time immemorial.

The king's lawyers did not dispute this claim but on further enquiry they discovered that John Gernon II had overcharged those using both the market and the fair. Edward III therefore took away these privileges from Gernon, though they were soon restored on the latter's payment of a fine of 40 shillings (£2).

Whether of three or 15 days' duration, Bakewell's fair must have been a remarkable occasion, when the town was visited by acrobats and jugglers, minstrels and dancers, strolling players and singers, quite apart from those who came to sell exotic foods, fruit and spices that were not seen at the weekly markets. How uninteresting is the modern-day fair, both as a spectacle and as a communal attraction.

Markets were of one day's duration and, by the late Middle Ages at least, were spread out in the streets of the town. Corn, butter, cheese and foodstuffs were sold below the church in what is now King Street. Livestock was sold in the streets, cattle and sheep in what is now the Square, horses towards the ford in the river and pigs at the foot of what is now North Church Street.

In the Middle Ages a trumpet or horn was blown to allow trading to commence and by the late-sixteenth century a market bell was rung at 11.00a.m. This seemingly late hour was set to allow traders travelling long distances to arrive and display their wares and to prevent forestalling. Indeed, market wardens in the lord's employ were ever watchful and reported any wrongdoing to the manor courts. Thus fines or future exclusion were imposed on those innkeepers who watered their ale, on traders who gave short measure and on the rogues and

vagabonds who inevitably mingled with the crowds.

There was no police force in the modern sense and parish constables, assisted by manorial officers and tell-tale Bakewellians, helped to keep the town 'clean' in every sense of the word. Those who fouled the town's water courses with their dunghills or who washed their dirty clothes at the wells were brought before the manorial courts. Those who blasphemed or were guilty of lewd behaviour were dealt with by the church authorities.

Though the manor courts generally maintained peace and security in the town one must not overlook the occasional lawlessness visited upon it from the outside. Control of such disorders was the duty of the county's Sheriff aided, in extreme cases, by an armed and mounted posse. The pursuit of felons in the Peak was not unlike the task confronting later Sheriffs in the Wild West. Everyone has heard of the mayhem and terror inflicted on the state of Missouri by the James brothers in the 1870s, but who has heard of the story of the Coterels in the Peak at the beginning of the fourteenth century?

Some of the facts can be gleaned from the Middleton Papers, published by the Historical Manuscripts Commission in 1911. James Coterel and his brothers, Nicholas and John, may well have come from the parish, if not the town, of Bakewell. Certainly a good number of their confederates were obviously local men, Robert le Savage, Stephen de Edensor, Nicholas de Calton, William de Buxton and William de Eyam. This marauding gang rode armed to the teeth, as to war, and committed thefts, burglaries, beatings and murders. They terrorised two counties, from Nottingham to Newark and from Derby through Wirksworth to Bakewell and into the Peak. Calling themselves *la compagnie sauvage*, they organised what today might be termed a protection racket. Letters were addressed to various wealthy victims, in the style of a royal command, requesting considerable sums of money. Failure to pay resulted in the recipient's house being burgled. The gang often stole their victims' arms and armour, doubtless with the intention of equipping themselves for further brigandage. Some, who did not pay promptly, were severely beaten and murders were committed in Ashbourne, Brassington and Wirksworth.

Markets and fairs were particular targets and prosperous merchants were snatched and held for intolerable ransoms. One such was Ralph Murimouth at Bakewell, who paid 100 shillings (£5), a considerable sum, to save his life.

The gang had no compunction in exploiting the clergy. The vicar of Youlgreave handed over 20 shillings (£1) for fear of his life and, along with the vicar of Markeaton, provided sustenance and a safe hiding place in return for protection. The courts duly accused these hapless clerics of harbouring and assisting notorious outlaws.

To protect his church, clergy and parishioners the vicar of Bakewell, Robert Bernard, sheltered the Coterel gang and sent food to their hideout in nearby Shacklow Woods. In doing so the vicar had the backing of the Dean and Chapter of Lichfield, two of whose canons lived in Bakewell as clergy at the church.

Gradually the gang's strength and activities diminished as its members were apprehended, tried and hanged. Although not recorded, this was presumably the fate of the Coterels themselves. As for the vicar of Bakewell, the Sheriff presented him before the king's justices accused of knowingly harbouring outlaws, and his lands, goods and chattels were forfeit to the Crown. As a priest he was allowed to plead his case in the archdiocesan court of York, where the archbishop found him innocent. His goods were restored to him, though he does not appear to have been reinstated as vicar of Bakewell.

So the town of Bakewell grew and developed during the two centuries of Gernon lordship and within the town and the manor a community of freemen and burgesses (those residing in the town) began to grow. Apart from holding parcels of freehold land they operated as lead, wool and corn merchants and were the precursors of a future professional class which included lawyers, apothecaries and shopkeepers. A remarkable document survives in the archives at Belvoir Castle, dated 1286, which outlines the liberties granted to them by Sir William Gernon.

A freeman or burgess of Bakewell could graze his cattle freely on the common and the moors and even enjoy free pasturage with the lord's cattle and sheep on the lord's lands, once any hay or corn had been taken in. He could freely take turf, heather and bracken from the moors for fuel and roofing material. Unlike the villeins, he was permitted to fish in the River Wye free from arrest for poaching. In the town he was not charged a toll to sell goods in either the weekly Monday market or the annual fair. He could brew ale, full and sell cloth and bake bread which he could freely sell. Nor was he compelled, as were others, to grind his corn at the lord's mill in Bakewell. If he flouted any manorial rules the courts fined him a flat rate of 3d. (1p) for each misdemeanour. Even if he committed bloodshed his fine was only 5s.4d. (26½p). The lord even helped him to pursue his own debtors and abusers, and made his prison available for holding such offenders until the Sheriff could conduct them to the Assizes.

In short, the freemen and burgesses of Bakewell were quite advanced in their privileges, which has led some to believe that the town became a borough in the late Middle Ages. However, no charter of incorporation has ever been found or referred to; the town remained firmly in the lord's control and is referred to as a vill in deeds of the fourteenth and fifteenth centuries.

After the Gernons

Following the death of Sir John Gernon in 1383/4 his lands were divided between his two daughters and co-heiresses, Joan and Margaret. For the next 120 years the manor of Bakewell passed by inheritance through the hands of the Swinburnes, Helions, Tirrells and Wentworths. All these families, like the Gernons before them, were Essex landowners. They have left no mark on Bakewell's history.

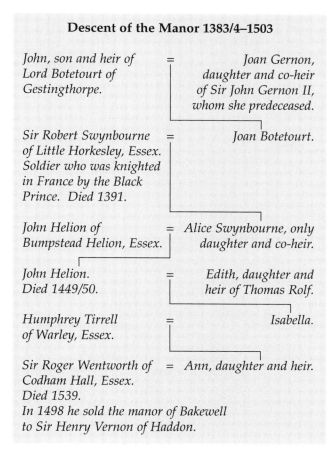

Descent of the Manor 1383/4–1503

John, son and heir of Lord Botetourt of Gestingthorpe.	=	Joan Gernon, daughter and co-heir of Sir John Gernon II, whom she predeceased.
Sir Robert Swynbourne of Little Horkesley, Essex. Soldier who was knighted in France by the Black Prince. Died 1391.	=	Joan Botetourt.
John Helion of Bumpstead Helion, Essex.	=	Alice Swynbourne, only daughter and co-heir.
John Helion. Died 1449/50.	=	Edith, daughter and heir of Thomas Rolf.
Humphrey Tirrell of Warley, Essex.	=	Isabella.
Sir Roger Wentworth of Codham Hall, Essex. Died 1539. In 1498 he sold the manor of Bakewell to Sir Henry Vernon of Haddon.	=	Ann, daughter and heir.

If the Gernons and their successors were largely absentee, more important lords than they were beginning to have an impact on Bakewell's development in the fourteenth and fifteenth centuries. These were the Foljambes, the Wensleys and the Vernons, who held manors within the parish. Under their patronage in the two centuries before the Reformation the Parish Church of All Saints achieved its final architectural grandeur.

A Foljambe probably came over with William the Conqueror and by the twelfth century the Foljambe family was established in the Peak with its principal seat at Tideswell. One branch acquired lands in and around Bakewell parish at Burton, Hassop, Darley, Stanton, Edensor and beyond. Sir Godfrey Foljambe was the most important member of this branch; he was seneschal to Sir John of Gaunt, constable of the High Peak, second baron of the Exchequer and chief steward of the Duchy of Lancaster. It is a testimony

Left: *Chantry monument of Sir Godfrey Foljambe and his wife in Derbyshire alabaster, 1385.*

Below: *The fourteenth-century font in front of the west door, c.1885. It was moved in 1890 to its present position at the west end of the south aisle.*

Above, left and right: *Detail of the figures of Saints Peter and Paul.*

Bakewell chantry house just before it was rebuilt.
(ENGRAVING BY RICHARD GODFREY, 1781)

The arms of Vernon and Pype on the church battlements, dating from the fifteenth century.

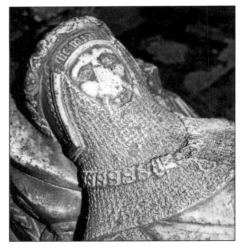

Detail from the effigy of Sir Thomas de Wensley, or Wendesley, in the Newark, 1403.

The fourteenth-century octagonal belfry and spire before the latter's removal in 1820.

(FROM AN ANONYMOUS OIL PAINTING, C.1819)

Urinating gargoyle (fourteenth century) at Haddon Hall.

to Sir Godfrey's standing in and beyond Bakewell that in 1360 Sir John Gernon leased the manor of Bakewell to him. Perhaps Sir John, who had no male heir, considered that Sir Godfrey might eventually purchase the manor, though both lease and purchase would have required royal consent since Bakewell was held in chief of the Crown. In the event Sir Godfrey died in 1377 and the manor reverted to Sir John, who died in 1384.

Just as Thomas Foljambe was a great benefactor to nearby Tideswell church, the 'Cathedral of the Peak' in which his monument is to be found, so Sir Godfrey's memorial commemorates his part in the embellishment of Bakewell church and the chantry of the Holy Cross, which he founded in 1344 and where he and his wife were interred. Initially the chantry priest appears to have lodged in a building where the old Town Hall now stands and here, too, the guild met and had a small chapel dedicated to St Mary – opposite St Mary's well. By the end of the fifteenth century, however, the two chantries, that of the Virgin and the older one of the Holy Cross, merged and used the Chantry House at the top of what is now North Church Street.

Much interior refurbishing took place in the church. Apart from the screens, fragments of which survive, the chancel was given new priests' stalls with finely carved misericordes (tilting seats) and poppy heads (stall or bench ends). Again, fragments survive in the chancel and the baptistry following the nineteenth-century restoration. The finest surviving item, however, is the stone tub font, octagonal in form, with a carved standing figure beneath a crocketed canopy on each face. As befits the church's

dedication to All Saints, Christ stands between the Virgin and St John the Divine, and Saints Peter and Paul, a mitred bishop (St Chad of Lichfield?), an unidentified priest-like figure and St John the Baptist occupy the other five sides.

The building, improved both without and within during the fourteenth century, became one of the finest churches in the county. A new octagonal bell chamber was ingeniously placed on the squat thirteenth-century tower – daring enough considering the weak Norman foundations and the steeply sloping site. As if this were too modest a feat, a peal of eight bells was hoisted into the octagon, which in turn was surmounted by an elegant octagonal stone spire. The parishioners were extremely proud of their bells, which were rung on every possible occasion. Amazingly, the construction of tower, octagon and spire stood for almost five centuries.

The 'Newark', or south transept, was given an eastern aisle by removing the old east wall, inserting arches and creating three chapels with altars, piscinae and carved oak screens. The southernmost appears to have given better accommodation for the chantry of the Virgin, whilst the northern one, towards the crossing, allowed for the new chantry dedicated to the Holy Cross

After Sir Godfrey Foljambe's death his family faded from the Bakewell area and a collateral branch established itself at Walton, near Chesterfield. The vacuum was to some extent filled by Sir Thomas de Wendesley, or Wensley. He held lands in and around Bakewell, at Darley, Winster, Wensley and elsewhere. A strong supporter of the Lancastrian cause at the end of the fifteenth century, he was constable and bailiff of the Duchy of Lancaster's lands within the High Peak. Of some repute as a soldier, his rather mutilated military effigy in the Newark of the church shows him wearing the Lancastrian collar of esses (from Henry Bolingbroke's motto of *souveraignté*),

The great hall at Haddon. Notice the incorrect eighteenth-century roof timbers, which were replaced with more authentic work in 1923.

whilst the brow of his helmet is embossed with 'IHC Nazaren' (Jesus of Nazareth). The latter may have saved his soul but failed to prevent his dying of wounds after the battle of Shrewsbury in 1403. He was probably a member of one or both of the chantry guilds and so was interred in the central chapel of the Newark's new east aisle.

For the rest of the fifteenth century and into the beginning of Elizabeth I's reign the most important family in the area was that of Vernon of Haddon. Sir Richard Vernon (d.1451) was steward of the Duchy of Lancaster's lordship of High Peak from 1424 and Sheriff of Nottinghamshire and Derbyshire from 1424 to 1426. He represented Derbyshire in the parliaments of 1422, 1426 (when he was Speaker) and 1433, and Henry VI appointed him Treasurer of Calais from 1445 to 1451. His son, Sir William, succeeded him in the above offices and became Constable of England.

Again, Bakewell Parish Church bears witness to the patronage of the wealthy Vernons. It was Sir William and his wife, Margaret Swynfen, who, perhaps in celebration of their marriage (1435), paid for the raising of the nave walls to incorporate clerestory windows whilst lowering the pitch of the fourteenth-century roof. Their joint coats of arms are still visible, carved on the newly added nave battlements. The church, like their hall at Haddon, was assuming a sham military appearance. It was probably they, too, who added the south porch with its low pitched roof and battlements to match the nave.

The son of Sir William, Sir Henry Vernon, was the most illustrious member of his family and the most interesting lord of Haddon. This courtly knight had the respect of the Yorkist kings, Edward IV and Richard III, and of their Lancastrian successor, Henry VII. Sir Henry had married Anne, daughter of John Talbot, second Earl of Shrewsbury and was in high favour at the court of Henry Tudor; so much so that the king appointed him a Knight of the Bath and governor and treasurer of Arthur, Prince of Wales.

Local historians write about how the young boy prince spent much time at Haddon Hall and Bakewell, how he had a vision at nearby Hassop crossroads foretelling his forthcoming marriage to Catherine of Aragon and his premature death, and how his shield now hangs in Bakewell church. All this is pure mythology and there is no evidence that he spent time at Bakewell or Haddon Hall.

His famous governor certainly did, and continued the family's benefactions to the church in Bakewell, endowing it in his will (1514) with a new rood-screen to carry the Crucifixion, with the Virgin and St John. He also paid for a chantry priest to say Masses for the salvation of his soul and those of his family in his chapel at Haddon. With the approach of the Reformation, neither of these benefactions would have survived much beyond the middle of the sixteenth century.

Slightly more enduring, in a secular sense, was Sir Henry's acquisition of Bakewell in 1498. In fact he purchased it from the absentee Wentworths for £724. At that date the manor consisted of 10 messuages, (i.e. dwellings with attached land and appurtenances), 50 acres of land, 100 acres of meadow, 300 acres of pasture, 40 acres of wood, 1,000 acres of gorse, heather and marsh, and 100s. of rent in Bakewell and Darley. This gives us a good idea of the extent of the varying types of land in Bakewell four centuries after the compilation of the Domesday Book.

However, Henry VII's lawyers intervened to hold up the sale, pointing out that since the days of the Gernons Bakewell had been held in chief of the king and was therefore, technically speaking, still a royal manor. Although Sir Henry Vernon's standing at court was high he still had to sue out his pardon and pay a fine of £40 before he could take possession. Thus, at the end of the Middle Ages, the manor of Bakewell was joined with Haddon under the Vernons and was ruled by the courts leet and baron held at Haddon Hall. The population of the town was now approaching 1,000 and that of the parish at least twice that number. Both town and parish were the largest in the High and Low Peak and Bakewell market was the most prosperous.

CHAPTER 3

From Vernon to Manners

Sir George Vernon, 'a Petty King in the Peak'

By the beginning of the Tudor period the Vernons had developed Haddon Hall into a double quadrangular house with a north-western entrance tower to match the Norman one at the south-east. The carriage entrance beneath the latter tower gave access to the upper, service court; the pedestrian passage, by steps beneath the lower tower, led into the residential court. Around this were disposed the chapel, the great hall and its kitchens and the parlour – a model of a late-medieval manor-house.

Here was maintained a resident household of some 40 servants augmented by daily employees brought in from Bakewell and the surrounding villages when the family and its guests were in residence. The household was largely self sufficient, producing meat from its own sheep, pigs and cattle, much of which was salted, powdered and spiced for winter use. From the cereal crops, largely grown on the Vernons's more prosperous Midland manors, flour was milled for bread, malt was produced for ale and beer, and oats for human and horse food.

Fruit was provided by the orchards at Haddon which grew on the slope between the Hall and the River Wye. Vegetables were grown in a kitchen garden, probably located across the river; there is evidence that onions, parsnips, peas and beans were grown. Fish were taken from the river and game from the park.

Sea fish, fresh and salted, came from Hull by river to Bawtry and then overland by packhorse to Chesterfield, Bakewell and so to Haddon Hall. Barrels of oysters and mussels from Whitstable were brought to Ashbourne on the London wagon and then over the hills by packhorse to Haddon. Wine was imported similarly from London and Hull; the lord and his family drank Rhenish wines from Germany, Burgundy and Bordeaux (claret) from France and sack (sherry) from Spain.

Luxury and exotic items were secured for the household by sending out sumpter horses to the fairs at Lenton, near Nottingham, Lichfield, Tamworth

Aerial view, taken in 1953, of Haddon Hall at its fullest extent. The brew house was removed at the end of the eighteenth century. It had adjoined the kitchens at the spot marked X.

Table tomb of Sir George Vernon and his two wives, Margaret (left) and Matilda (right), 1567, Bakewell church.

Sir George Vernon, aged three, on the monument of his father Richard in St Bartholomew's at Tong, Shropshire.

and elsewhere. At least once a year the lord of Haddon and his caterer made journeys to London, often on legal business, but also to buy special products only obtainable there.

Into this busy, thriving household and lordship, in 1514, was born George, last male heir of the Vernons of Haddon. He was the only son of Richard, who succeeded his father, Sir Henry, in 1515. Richard himself died two years later and the infant George inherited the Vernon estates as a minor at the age of three. His mother married twice more, first to Sir William Coffin of Devon and, on his death, to Sir Richard Manners, brother of Thomas Manners, 1st Earl of Rutland. This marriage thus established a link between the Vernon and Manners families well before the supposed elopement of Dorothy Vernon and John Manners early in the reign of Elizabeth I.

The infant George was placed in the wardship of his uncle John and at 14 was studying at Magdalen College, Oxford. Two images of George Vernon survive; first, the lone effigy of a young boy in early-Tudor dress standing at the foot of his father's tomb in Tong church; second, a venerable, bearded old man, in plate armour and heraldic tabard, reclining between his two wives in the Newark of Bakewell church.

This man left more romantic memories – and myths – among the people of the Peak than any lord of Bakewell before or since. He cut a fine figure on his white horse caparisoned in black, his armorial colours. He distributed alms to the poor after

Haddon Hall c.1895, showing the north-west entrance tower, c.1530, with stables at the bottom of the hill.

attending Mass at All Saints' Church and sent doles to the beggars who clamoured at the gates of Haddon Hall. He was knighted at the coronation of Edward VI in 1547 and the Elizabethan historian, Sir William Camden, famously said of him:

For the magnificent port [deportment] *that he carried, the open house that he kept and his commendable hospitality,* [he] *got the name among the multitude of a Petty King in the Peak.*

Sir George was not just the last male heir of his line but one of the last figures of the medieval period. Despite his time at Oxford he was not a bookish or scholarly knight and although his household accounts tell us of some interest in music and drama at Haddon Hall, this would appear to have been on the part of his first wife, Margaret (Taylboys), and of his daughters, Margaret and Dorothy. So in 1553 we find him bringing home from London a number of lute strings and on May Day 1559 he invited 'Lord Willoughby's new players' to entertain the family in a springtime masque, or play. Though admitted to Gray's Inn in 1537 he never intended to become a lawyer but enjoyed administering his estates, over which he hunted freely, as he did over those of his friends and neighbours. Nether Haddon village had decayed and been emparked and Burton, another of the original Domesday outliers of Bakewell, had similarly vanished. The park at Haddon had grown by the end of the fifteenth century and extended from Bakewell along the Wye valley to Rowsley and into the Derwent valley as far as Darley; northwards from Haddon Hall itself, it stretched into Lathkil Dale beyond Alport and Over Haddon as far as Monyash, encompassing Bradford Dale between Winster and Youlgreave. Wild boar had been hunted to extinction and wolves had long been exterminated, but deer were plentiful and the great hall at Haddon still

Haddon Hall kitchens, fitted out for Sir George Vernon in the early-sixteenth century.

(Lithograph by Samuel Rayner, 1836)

displays their blanched antlers.

Rabbits abounded in the park's warrens and were taken by dogs, ferrets and nets. A considerable variety of birds was killed for feasts at the Hall, ranging from water-fowl and herons to snipe, plovers, larks and moorland grouse. All were either shot, netted or brought down by falcons. The household accounts tell us that Sir George even used an osprey for hunting.

The Rivers Wye, Lathkil and Bradford teemed with fish. William of Worcester, writing in the 1480s, tells us in dog Latin:

… in Wye water sunt pisces, trouthes [trout], *culleys* [miller's thumb], *loches* [loach], *anguillae* [eels], *graylynghes* [grayling], *boleheads* [bullheads], *penkys* [minnows], *et salmons* [salmon] *boni inter tempus vocate Seynt Mary dayes.*

Sir George's water bailiffs policed the River Wye and its tributaries and employed skilled servants to catch

27

the local delicacy, freshwater crayfish, which grew as big as prawns. Large pike were brought in from pools and rivers on his other manors, together with a range of freshwater fish.

Although Sir George toured his 30 or so manors, residing at Tong and Harleston, he gradually adopted Haddon Hall as his principal seat and Bakewell church as his place of worship. He embellished the Hall by panelling the parlour (built by his grandfather) with the carved arms of Henry VIII, Edward, Prince of Wales, his own and those of his ancestors. He also inserted the stained-glass armorials in the parlour window, making the decoration of this room amongst the most important of its date (1545) in England.

The great north-west tower was added by Sir George, together with the little postern gate beside it bearing his arms. He was responsible, too, for refurbishing the famous kitchens and for adding to them a brew house (which was demolished late in the eighteenth century). Not only were ale and beer brewed here but in the great alembic, or still, aqua vitae was distilled, together with a variety of herbal potions used by the household apothecary for medical treatment of the Vernon family and its servants.

Bakewell also had an apothecary in the sixteenth century; such men dispensed remedies, bled patients by applying leeches and performed minor surgery. Qualified doctors and surgeons had to be sent for from the nearest city. The poor of the town, naturally, could not afford the services of an apothecary and the rich could not speedily summon a surgeon. Even Sir George found his wealth of no avail when his first wife, Margaret, lay seriously ill at Haddon in 1558. He called the local apothecary from Bakewell and then summoned the one from Chesterfield. Neither could halt his wife's decline. In desperation he despatched a servant to bring Dr Slynderhurst from Oxford. Sadly, a second servant was sent to intercept and pay the doctor at Southam, in Warwickshire. Lady Vernon had died, leaving Sir George with two young daughters of marriageable age.

His life had been full of disappointments, one of which was his failure to be ennobled. In 1547 Lord Paget had presented to the ailing Henry VIII a list of prospective peers which included Sir George's name, but the king died before he could sign it. Indeed, between 1543 and 1552 Sir George was nominated for a peerage nine times without success. The reasons for this, religious or otherwise, are not clear. Now without a male heir, Sir George married within six weeks Matilda, or Maude, Longford of Longford in south Derbyshire. He had no further offspring and sought eligible husbands for his two daughters, who would divide his wide estates between them. His elder daughter, Margaret, was married in 1558 to Sir Thomas Stanley of Winwick in Lancashire, second son of Edward, Earl of Derby. On Sir George's death his Staffordshire and Shropshire estates, centred on

Mural monument of Sir John Manners (d.1611) and his wife, Dorothy Vernon (d.1584), on the south wall of the Newark.

Tong, went to Sir Thomas.

The marriage of his younger daughter, Dorothy, has spawned half a dozen romantic 'novels' of no literary merit and an opera, *Haddon Hall*, set to music by Sir Arthur Sullivan. All are based on her purported elopement with John Manners, a suitor whom her father, we are told, despised. This story is no older than the 1820s and need not concern us here. John Manners was in fact a good match for Sir George's second daughter. He was the second son of Thomas Manners, 1st Earl of Rutland, to the family of whom Sir George was half related by his mother's third marriage.

Sir George died in 1565, leaving his Derbyshire estates, centred on Bakewell and Haddon Hall, to Dorothy and John. He himself was buried in the Newark of Bakewell church. He reclines between his two wives on a tomb chest in the newly rearranged Vernon chapel.

The Reformation

If Sir George, like the Peverils, Avenels, Gernons and Foljambes before him, represented the old Anglo-Norman families, the sixteenth century saw the rise of a new generation of landed gentry not of direct

Norman descent. Such were the Suffolk knight William Cavendish and his wife, Bess of Hardwick, who purchased the Chatsworth estate in 1547. They began to build the new 'high rise' Chatsworth House, the first 'country house' in the north. What a contrast this was to Sir George's sprawling medieval accretions at Haddon, only two and a half miles away.

Another parvenu family acquiring land in and around Bakewell was that of the Gells of Hopton, near Wirksworth. In contrast to the Vernons, the Gells were villeins as late as the early-fifteenth century. The founder of their fortunes was Ralph Gell, Principal of Clement's Inn, who profited from his legal practice and from lead and sheep on his growing Derbyshire estates.

Both the Cavendishes and the Gells were Protestants and profited above all from the Reformation. Sir William Cavendish made a fortune from his part in the Dissolution of the Monasteries; Ralph Gell advantageously purchased the farm of church tithes (the right to collect them) in the High and the Low Peak, including those of Bakewell, from the Dean and Chapter of Lichfield.

Sir George Vernon, the last male heir of a devout Catholic family, must have viewed with some bewilderment the rapid pace of religious change as he lived through the reigns of Henry VIII, Edward VI and Mary and into that of Elizabeth I. He must have regarded the way others profited from the Church's disarray with some alarm. He quietly, and perhaps reluctantly, went along with the changes. In 1546 he was appointed one of the commissioners to dissolve the college of priests in Tong church, together with the chantry there. He also helped dissolve the chantries in Bakewell church. Interestingly, the endowment lands of these institutions were purchased by his stepfather, Sir Richard Manners. By the end of his life, his work as deputy lieutenant and Justice of the Peace within Derbyshire indicates that he was a trusted official. In 1564 Thomas Bentham, Bishop of Lichfield and Coventry, considered him 'a great justice [in] religion as in all other things.'

Conversely, those who refused to give up the Catholic faith in Bakewell's far-flung parish had two options; they could either face fines and even imprisonment or they could conform to the new Protestant rites, whilst secretly harbouring priests to celebrate Mass in their concealed, makeshift domestic chapels. The Eyres of Hassop, two miles from Bakewell, were excellent examples of the latter. They continued to attend the chapel of ease at Great Longstone whilst surreptitiously holding Mass in their house at Hassop. Such crypto-Catholics were known as church papists.

It was the task of the lord lieutenant of the county, the Earl of Shrewsbury from Sheffield Castle, assisted by his deputy lieutenants and the JPs, to deal with the Catholic recusants (those refusing to attend the Elizabethan church services) and to hunt down the Catholic priests. In 1588, at nearby Padley Hall, a house of Derbyshire's two most prominent Catholic families, the Eyres and the Fitzherberts, the lord lieutenant's officers pounced. Father Nicholas Garlick and Father Robert Ludlam, discovered there, were tried and then hanged, drawn and quartered at Derby. Sir Thomas Fitzherbert and his son John both died in prison.

Bakewell church, once the glory of the Peak, bore physical witness to the Protestant onslaught. In 1534, having first stopped payments of church taxes and then clerical appeals to Rome, Parliament declared Henry VIII Supreme Head of the Church of England. In Bakewell church, as elsewhere, images or arms of 'the bishop of Rome' (i.e. the Pope) were removed and the arms of the king and those of his Protestant successors replaced them. Bakewell church still displays the arms of Queen Anne, the Protestant daughter of the Catholic James II. Thomas Cromwell's Injunctions of 1536 and 1538 decreed that images and shrines should be taken down and these, no doubt, accounted for the destruction of the rood and the removal of stained glass with images of Christ and his saints. Amazingly, the fine medieval font escaped mutilation. In 1550 an Injunction of Edward VI called for the ejection of altars with their five dedicational crosses representing Christ's five wounds. In their place came plain wooden communion tables to be spread with a simple linen cloth on which the commemorative last supper was celebrated. One such table survived in Bakewell church until stolen in the 1980s.

On the accession of Edward VI, an Act was passed abolishing colleges of priests and chantry chapels and the guilds. At a stroke the chantry and college priests of All Saints' Church were dismissed, the chapels of the Virgin and of the Holy Cross were dissolved and their endowments confiscated. The control of the Dean and Chapter of Lichfield over Bakewell church

Left: *Ralph Gell of Hopton, lawyer, and his two wives, 1564, on an incised stone slab in St Mary's Church, Wirksworth. He built the Parsonage House in Bakewell soon after 1534.*

(SCRAPER BOARD BY TREVOR BRIGHTON)

The Parsonage House in 1955. The Harrison family gave it to the newly formed Bakewell & District Historical Society in 1954. Miss Pitt was its last occupant, continuing to live in her parents' tenement until 1966.

(WATERCOLOUR BY THE LATE GEORGE BUTLER FRWS OF CASTLE STREET, BAKEWELL, 1955)

The site of St John's Hospital, founded in 1602. The almshouses shown here were rebuilt in the garden in 1709.

The Market Hall at the end of the nineteenth century, when it served as a Town Hall upstairs and a laundry beneath. The filled-in arcades of the original building are just visible and are exposed inside.

The Market Hall as it might have looked in its heyday.

(DRAWING BY FRANK SAUNDERS)

was largely reduced to the appointment of a vicar and curate.

Indeed, the Dean and Chapter, like other cathedral authorities, quaked as Henry VIII surveyed sources of Church income. Lichfield leased its farming of tithes in the Peak to Ralph Gell in 1534. As part of the agreement Gell was required to build a parsonage house (i.e. a tithe collector's house) and tithe barn just to the west of Bakewell church. Then, as royal pressure increased, the Dean and Chapter sold both the right to collect the tithes and the parsonage house (now the Old House Museum) to Gell.

Poverty and Prosperity in the Parish and Town

Tithes, originally a tenth of the produce of those within the parish who worked the land, had been paid since Saxon times to maintain the Parish Churches and their clergy and to help the poor, and their transfer from ecclesiastical to lay authorities, as at Bakewell, was a considerable economic and social blow. As the population grew so did the numbers of the unemployed, the sick, the vagrants and the beggars. Locally levied rates were sorely needed to tackle the problem. Enclosure Acts were partly to blame for depriving the labouring classes, once the strip-owning villeins, of a stake in the old manorial field system. Bakewell must have suffered less than most in this regard, since its fields were not fully enclosed until the early-nineteenth century. Inflation and a rise in prices, whilst allowing some to prosper, hit the labouring poor hard.

By piecemeal Poor Law legislation in 1536, 1563 and 1572 the government strove to address a problem it barely understood. In 1601 it tried to tidy up earlier efforts in the Poor Law Act of that year, which placed the obligation to administer poor relief firmly on the Parish Vestry. It was the duty of the churchwardens to collect obligatory parish dues, assessed by the local JPs, from the better-off parishioners so that the money could be used to support the infirm and the children. The able-bodied unemployed received no relief and beggars and vagrants were dealt with, often harshly, by the parish constable. Men were compelled to complete their apprenticeships and remain in low paid employment within the parish, if possible.

Philanthropic endowments by wealthy members

Dovecote at Haddon Hall, dated 1614, which provided eggs and birds for the kitchen. Inside are nesting recesses for about 1,000 pigeons and roosting spaces for as many more.

of society brought additional relief. In Bakewell in 1602 John Manners founded and built St John's Hospital by the south-east gate of the churchyard. Originally the hospital consisted of four dwellings, to which were added, three years later, two further lodgings and a dining hall. The site was that of an old chapel which was probably part of the house of St Mary's chantry, across the road (King Street) from St Mary's well. The accommodation was for four poor, single men of the parish, who wore gowns with a yellow and blue cross on the left breast. Above the lodgings was built a Town Hall and court room, the former to allow for Vestry and other town meetings, the latter to enable the JPs to hold their annual Quarter Sessions. John Manners had thus given the town a hall for local government and established an important centre for charitable relief.

Indeed, he prospered considerably from the profits on lead and sheep and, following the premature death in 1584 of his wife Dorothy, he never married again, devoting himself to the upbringing of his children, to his legal and administrative duties in the county and to the welfare and expansion of Bakewell. To him we must attribute the new Market Hall, built about the same time as the hospital, an indication of Bakewell's late-Elizabethan prosperity. Although today it has been altered beyond recognition, old photographs reveal that it was a typical arcaded structure on the ground floor, with a windowed storey above, a larger version, in fact, of that which in part survives at neighbouring Winster, and which is currently owned by the National Trust.

John Manners's wealth was also reflected in the last building phase at Haddon Hall. Here, to modernise his house and try to keep abreast of the new developments at nearby Chatsworth, he employed the important Elizabethan architect Robert Smithson. Wollaton Hall, near Nottingham, Hardwick Hall and Bolsover's Little Castle were among Smithson's achievements; at Haddon Hall he designed the splendid Long Gallery and the renowned terraced garden, with its bowling green and lovely steps. John's wife, Dorothy, had died before the work was finished, so all her associations with the gallery and the garden belong to nineteenth-century romantic mythology.

In 1603, when John Manners joined the local gentry and aristocracy at Worksop to welcome the Scots king, James VI, on his way south to be crowned as James I of England, the king knighted him. Lord of Bakewell for 45 years, John Manners died in 1611 and was buried beside his wife in the Newark. There they rested beneath their large mural monument until their disinterment in 1840 as a result of the rebuilding of the church. Sir George, their eldest son, married Grace Pierrepoint but died in 1624 to be succeeded in turn by his son, John. During their lordships, in the 30 years before the Civil War, Bakewell expanded further. To this period belong the building of the Mercers' Hall, the establishment of the Bath House and the foundation of Lady Manners School.

Haddon Hall's Long Gallery, designed by Robert Smithson and built c.1589.

(LITHOGRAPH BY SAMUEL RAYNER, 1836)

Haddon Hall, c.1900. The terrace garden was designed by Robert Smithson in the 1580s.

The Clothing Hall in front of the old market place. Erected in the second half of the seventeenth century, it was demolished in 1936. (TRADE CARD, LATE-NINETEENTH CENTURY)

The Mercers' Hall, known variously as the Woollen Hall and the Clothing Hall, was erected on the side of the old market place. Who built this fine four-storey building, and when, is unknown. It appears to have been mercers' shops and houses and perhaps contained their hall. It was certainly a statement about their standing in the commercial life of Bakewell, though sadly it was pulled down in 1936 and replaced with a so-called replica.

The earliest reference to a bathing place in Bakewell belongs to 1637, when John Manners built an enclosure around the chalybeate spring known as the Town Well (on the site of the present Bath House). Inspired, no doubt, by the Earl of Shrewsbury's restoration of Buxton's baths, the Bakewell bath was initially intended for the private use of the Manners family and friends. It appears to have been open to the elements though not to public view.

Of great importance was the foundation in 1636 of Lady Manners School. Grace, the widow of Sir George Manners, had concerned herself with charity in Bakewell and especially with St John's Hospital. Her indenture granted an income of £15 a year from parcels of land:

> *... for the mayntayning of a schoolemaster for ever to teach a free schoole within the Towneshippe of Bakewell... for the better instructing of the male Children of the Inhabitants of Bakewell and Greate Rowsley... in good learneinge and Christian religion.*

The school was originally set up in one of the thatched cottages on the south side of the churchyard, though today it is a large comprehensive school on the western edge of the town. Pupils still celebrate the foundation by laying a chaplet of flowers on Lady Manners's monument, a huge Jacobean whatnot with figures of her, Sir George and their nine children.

Their first son having died at birth, it was their second, John, who succeeded to the estates centred on Bakewell and Haddon on the death of his father.

Lady Manners, founder of Lady Manners School.

In 1641, however, when his cousin George, 7th Earl of Rutland, died childless, he inherited the huge Belvoir estates in Leicestershire and Lincolnshire and the title of 8th Earl. Thereafter Belvoir, not Haddon, became his family's premier seat.

The Civil War

In the 1620s and 1630s Bakewell, like most towns, sullenly paid the taxes levied upon it by Charles I, though it found the 'Anglo-Catholicism' promoted by the Archbishop William Laud hard to stomach. Its clergy and parish upheld a more moderate form of Anglicanism. When war between king and parliament broke out in 1642 the town was largely Parliamentarian in sympathy. To a large degree it followed the stance taken by its lord, the 8th Earl of Rutland. He had served as High Sheriff of Derbyshire and had the irksome duty of collecting taxes at a time when Charles I ruled without parliament. He sat as an MP for the county in the Short Parliament of 1640 and viewed with dismay its peremptory dismissal by the king. He could be described as a 'low Anglican' in terms of churchmanship and had some sympathy with Puritanism. Charles I appointed him a deputy lieutenant of the county in 1640 and in 1642 preferred him over William Cavendish, Earl of Devonshire, as its lord

A photograph c.1900 showing the thatched cottage in South Church Street (second from the top) *traditionally said to be the first location of Lady Manners School.*

lieutenant. It was too late to win his loyalty. Rutland was one of only 22 peers who remained at Westminster when the king moved his council and court to York.

The story of Sir John Gell, grandson of Ralph, whom we have met earlier, is similar. He had served as Sheriff in 1635 and was made a JP and deputy lieutenant but his animosity towards the king grew, as did his leanings towards Puritanism and Presbyterianism. As a final sop the king awarded him a baronetcy in 1642 and he promptly joined the parliamentary cause, recruiting in Bakewell and in the High and Low Peak to raise a regiment of horse and foot. Robert Devereux, Earl of Essex and parliament's commander-in-chief, made him Governor of Derby and commander of the county's parliamentary forces.

If the highly taxed shopkeepers and wool merchants of the town and parish were generally of the parliamentary persuasion, some, especially those of high Anglican or Catholic conscience, found Royalist leadership in the Cavendish family at Chatsworth and Bolsover Castle. Chief among these was Rowland Eyre of Hassop, the grandson of Rowland, the wily church Papist.

All these families, Manners, Cavendish, Gell and Eyre, owed a good part of their wealth to the lucrative lead ore beneath their estates. Their income was derived in taxes from the free miners who extracted the lead and from the merchants who sent it by packhorse via Chesterfield to Bawtry and thence by river to Hull and by sea to the Continent. Lead merchants were generally prosperous at this time and Parliamentarian in allegiance. Such was Bernard Wells, a lead merchant from the Forest of Dean, who moved to Bakewell in 1620 and built a fine house at Holme. Another was William Savile of nearby Beeley

Mural monument of Sir George Manners (d.1623) and Grace Pierrepoint (d.1649) on the north wall of the Newark. Their second son, John, succeeded as 8th Earl of Rutland in 1641.

Hall, steward to the 8th Earl of Rutland, who looked after the earl's lead interests.

The lead miners themselves were not so predictable. Rough and rude in their manners and often living in hovels and even caves, they were very mobile in their work, having strings of hardy nags as mounts and packhorses. In towns like Bakewell they could be a scourge, frequenting the many alehouses that sprang up to quench their thirst. The JPs meeting in the town tried and failed to control them. The landowners found the miners hostile to paying their own taxes, let alone those due to the king. Rutland had many confrontations with them before and after the Civil War and on one occasion they threatened to burn Haddon Hall. Though some joined the king's Lifeguard when Prince Rupert came recruiting at nearby Tideswell in 1642, and others were conscripted as sappers in local regiments on both sides, they played no significant part in the war.

Nor did Bakewell. Cavendish forces were briefly billeted in the town in 1643 and its markets were virtually at the mercy of their nearby Royalist garrisons at Chatsworth and Hassop. However, after the Royalist defeat at Marston Moor in 1644 the Cavendishes had fled to the Continent, an ingloriously loyal and

Holme Hall, c.1910, built in 1626 for Gloucestershire lead merchant Bernard Wells. On the left is the older house.

spent force. Nor did the 8th Earl of Rutland distinguish himself. Having declared himself a Presbyterian and taken the Solemn League and Covenant in 1643, he was censured by parliament in 1645 for allowing the Bishop of Durham to sign his daughter with the cross at her baptism. His castle at Belvoir was occupied by Royalists and demolished by parliament. Given £1,500 as compensation, he reluctantly retired to his outmoded house, Haddon Hall, to await more settled times and an opportunity to rebuild his ancestral home.

Sir John Gell fared no better. Having been appointed Governor of Derby, he held the county for parliament until he was disgraced and briefly imprisoned in the Tower for his revived Royalist sympathies. Needless to say, at the Restoration in 1660, both Rutland and Gell worked their way back into royal favour, whilst a number of minor gentry families never recovered their old standing despite their steadfast loyalty to the king.

The Departure of the Manners Family

Bakewell had suffered no destruction in the Civil War unless it was further desecration of church furnishings by the soldiery. No medieval church plate survives; it was probably melted down for coinage to pay local regiments. It is significant that the oldest piece the church possesses is a chalice of 1670. Edward Browne, the future physician of Charles II, stayed in the town in 1662, probably at the Red Lion

or the White Horse, and described its run-down shops and houses thus:

We got to Bakewell – a little after dark – where at our Inne as it could not be expected sumptuous it was not halfe so bad as we might fear, for our host was very civill and gave us the best accommodations that Barren country could afford and therefore after we had drunk a gun of their good ale… up went a string with a piece of mutton and a chicken at the end of it… but our horses could not fare so well, no litter or oates, so they had to lay abroad in a cold rotten meadow. We squashed down on our seats amongst other townes-men. Our Darbishiere friend who joined us at the inne was clearly the local oracle. We had a merry night. Before a good fire we began to flea off our cloathes to dry ourselves but the natives they never put themselves to that trouble. I thinke, dry and wet is all one to them, they fear no weather and their common saying is 'when all is wet the skin will hold out yet'. We had the best bed in the house and I snorted out the night pretty well. This morning we walked up and down to see the Church and a hot bath and well which are here, but for want of looking after they have let the cold spring break in and mingle with the hot.

Their houses are most of them built without mortar, stones heaped upon stones make a substantial wall and by their own weight keep strong and fast. They cover their houses with a slate from local hills. The buildings are low and seem natural rather than artificial. Returning to the Inne we were accosted with the best musick the place could afford, an excellent Bagpipes.

The packhorse bridge at Holme (c.1664), with the ford on the upstream (north) side. The stables and dovecote of Holme Hall are on the left.

Bagshaw Hall and gardens, c.1920, built in 1686 for the attorney and steward to the Earl of Rutland, Thomas Bagshaw.

Top: *Inside the 1st Duke of Rutland's Bath House, and* (above) *the outside, from Bath Gardens.*

and Bakewell. The king had appointed him lord lieutenant of Leicestershire and he was deeply involved in the rebuilding of Belvoir Castle. This was completed in 1668, only to be destroyed by fire. The earl relied on his agent, the attorney Thomas Bagshaw, to regulate his affairs in and around Bakewell, especially in lead mining. In 1686 Bagshaw built himself a splendid house, stables and gardens to the north of the church looking across the town from what is now Bagshaw Hill.

The 8th Earl died in 1679 but was not interred in Bakewell church – nor were any later members of the Manners family. Instead his monument was erected in Bottesford church, by Belvoir Castle, the resting place of his noble ancestors. His chief legacies were the extensions and improvements made during his family's enforced stay at Haddon Hall. He extended Smithson's gardens down to the river and built two charming bridges across it – the first a new entrance bridge across the old ford; the second a pretty fishing bridge just outside the garden wall.

His son, the 9th Earl, was created Marquess of Granby and 1st Duke of Rutland by Queen Anne in 1703. By that date Belvoir was again rebuilt and the family had left Haddon, though he too had left a few additions to the gardens by adding an aviary and building a new bowling green and stand up the hill above the house in 1696. In Bakewell he improved and extended the Bath House in 1695 and ten years later he built a vault over the bath itself.

Lastly, in 1709, he rebuilt St John's Hospital and the Town Hall. The almshouses were reconstructed as a terrace housing six men, alongside the road and using what had been a garden for the earlier lodgings beneath the Town Hall. This last space was now opened out on the front as a butter market and the room above, the first Town Hall, was refurbished to double as a meeting room and a court. The royal arms had been placed behind the magistrates' bench in 1670, a new wooden dock could accommodate prisoners and steps led down on the outside to two cells. In front of the butter market the town stocks remained; the cuckstool for dunking loose-tongued women in the river was still in use and was repaired by the parish constable in 1723. Here was the real centre of the town until the Square was laid out in 1805, and the focal point of law and order until the police station was built in 1845 and the new Town Hall in 1890.

The town still lacked good communications and signposts, the drovers' lanes and packhorse tracks being the only routes through the parish. Edward Browne himself needed guides from Chesterfield to reach the town and in 1698 Celia Fiennes had difficulty covering the three miles from Chatsworth. Some improvements were made by replacing the wooden packhorse bridge at Lumford with one of stone in 1666 and the Parish Vestry did keep the town's streets and drains reasonably clean and well repaired.

The Earl of Rutland spent less time at Haddon

✦ CHAPTER 4 ✦

Georgian Bakewell: Towards a New Prosperity

Haddon Hall, engraved by François Vivares after Thomas Smith of Derby, 1743. The grounds are full of outgrown trees. The Manners family had left for Belvoir 40 years earlier.

Rural Peace and Economic Decline 1715–60

The departure of the Manners family was a social and economic blow to Bakewell. Not only had the town lost its focal point of patronage and leadership – a vacuum eventually filled to some degree by the Dukes of Devonshire – it also lost the benefits of Haddon Hall and its park. Both had brought employment to the townsfolk, whether it was by helping in the brew house, the kitchens, providing produce for the household or assisting with the hunt, gamekeeping or catching fish for the family. The Hall was locked and left in the charge of a steward, though this did not prevent thieves stealing fifteenth-century stained glass from the chapel's east window. The gardens gradually became bare and the trees overgrown as a lone gardener struggled to keep them trim, weed the courtyards, maintain the aviary and dovecote and feed the peacocks. The deer in the park had been killed off and the pack of otter hounds dispersed. The very trees in the park were purchased by William Thornhill of nearby Stanton Hall in 1724 and felled for making props in the local lead mines. William Archer of Holme Hall wrote to his brother in 1722 that 'Haddon Park is all demolished but ye H[ouse] which goes next!' Yet Haddon Hall survived, with the exception of Sir George Vernon's brew house.

If Haddon Hall slept in a cocoon for the next 200 years Bakewell, too, dozed in the first half of the eighteenth century. It was a lovely rural backwater where the farming round was still in tune with the rotation of crops in the unenclosed fields. Small farms still operated in the town itself, not yet in the fields, and livestock were a daily sight leaving the streets for the pastures and returning again for milking, dipping or slaughter. Hay and straw were stacked in countless barns and grain was ground at the mill.

The cattle markets filled the streets with even more livestock. Pigs were sold at the foot of North Church Street, horses near the town bridge and sheep and cows in front of the White Horse Inn. Fairs, though fewer in number now, were also held here until the First World War. Corn, butter, cheese, eggs and poultry were sold within and around the Market Hall in Bridge Street. Here, then, was one of the busiest livestock and stall markets in the county, haphazardly spread about the town. The numerous alehouses were the meeting places where farmers clinched their deals. There were only two inns in the town, the Red Lion and the White Horse (where now is the Rutland Arms), though the few tourists who came to see the Wonders of the Peak were generally unimpressed by their accommodation.

Intrepid traveller Celia Fiennes rode from Chesterfield via Chatsworth to Bakewell in 1698 and wrote in her diary:

Thence we came to Bankwell [Bakewell] a pretty neate market town, it stands on a hill yet you descend a vast hill to it, which you would thinke impossible to go down and we was forced to fetch a great compass, and by reason of the steepness and hazard of the Wayes – if you take a wrong Way there is no passing – you are forced to have Guides as in all parts of Darbyshire, and unless it be a few that use to be guides the common people know not above 2 or 3 mile from their home, but they of the country will climbe up and down with their horses those steep precipices; there are many fine springs of water purling out of the rocks on these hills; at Bankwell there was an excellent Minister in the Publick who pray'd and preach'd very seriously and his Life and Conversation is suitable, not very frequent in our dayes to be found; we went 3 mile off in the afternoone to heare another that was in a Meeteing and so 3 mile home againe; the hills about the town and all about the town is rocks of the finest marble of all sorts, huge rock, I took some of it and shewing it to severall they think it comparable to any beyond sea.

She was obviously impressed by the good living and preaching vicar of Bakewell. All Saints' Church was still very much the religious focal point of the town. Indeed, if one reads the idealised poem by William Archer of Holme Hall, written about 1720, there were no religious factions and the people lived in a blissful rural idyll.

Where pleasant Bakewell lifts its many heads,
With decent seats and trees so interwove,
It seems at once a village and a grove:
As if the plan from trading Belgia came,
Wey [the River Wye] ye canal and it ye Amsterdame
Not so with different opinions torn
For all live in that they all was born
And distant to ye realms of fell despight
A mutual amity does them unite
On given faith securely we depend
None meets his enemy but each his friend
Propounded truths as redily believe
Unskill'd in fraud and artless to deceave
But hospitably prone to doing good
Peace hovers ore ye tranquil neighbourhood.

These gentrified, utopian views by no means give the whole story. Bakewell may have been a delightful place to view and to live in – for some. The parish constables' accounts give us insight into the ordinary, even lowest, order of life.

The parish constable was elected from among the freemen and was a precursor of the modern 'bobby on the beat'. However, his duties extended well beyond issues of law and order. He was responsible to the JPs for its maintenance but was answerable to the Courts Leet and baron for policing the fields and meadows, to the Parish Vestry for maintaining the roads, footpaths and bridges and to the Sheriff and the lord lieutenant for taxation and military matters.

Thus we find the parish constable apprehending the numerous beggars and vagabonds who moved from parish to parish collecting free meals, accommodation and even rudimentary medical assistance. He would conduct them across the parish boundary with all speed. Bakewell's prison cells, located beside the Town Hall, were used to hold thieves, pickpockets and the violent. One of the cells was known as the cage, in which miscreants could be soundly thrashed. Women of ill repute were often whipped through the town and pregnant vagrants were hurried on lest the impending birth put the parish to further unwanted expense. Serious offenders were handed over to the Sheriff and the JPs.

The constable also policed the fields and meadows and kept down vermin with the aid of a crow shooter, a fox catcher and a moldewarper. He supervised the mending of gates, fences and church walls, the pinfold for stray or impounded livestock and the sheep wash at Lumford. From the packhorse bridge there to the site of the modern Meaden bridge (the approach to the Agricultural Centre) all crossings and fords over the Wye were kept in repair, as were the parish roads and steep causeways of the town at Bagshaw Hill and Fly Hill. The maintenance of the town wells was of particular importance since they were the town's water-supply, especially the Great Well (i.e. St Mary's well in present-day King Street), the steps to which were in regular need of repair.

Each year, in the summer, the constable ensured the principal wells of the town were dressed with bunches of flowers and blessed by the vicar on midsummer's day. This Christian celebration was a continuance of a pagan ritual originating in Celtic times, when wells were venerated. In Bakewell these well-dressing festivals were maintained until about 1753, died out until 1843, and have since been revived using religious tableaux made chiefly from flower petals.

The roads or tracks to and from Bakewell were particularly hazardous in hard winters and many tales are told of travellers losing their way on the Great Moor towards Sheffield and Chesterfield and even dying there. In 1697 the government authorised local JPs to order the erection of guide posts, or stoops, where crossroads were remote from towns and villages. The High Peak JPs took action in 1709 and instructed the local constables and overseers of the highways to erect gritstone stoops inscribed with directions to the nearest towns or villages. In Bakewell that year Charles Ellis made the stoops, John Wheeldon cut the signs on them and James Greaves had them erected. A few survive, notably the one above Edensor on the Bakewell road. Although they stood some six feet above the ground, severe winters could obliterate them. In 1725, for instance, we find the constables' road workers 'cutting a way through snow' to prevent Bakewell from being marooned.

Recruiting, equipping and paying local volunteers for the militia was also the parish constable's duty. He kept a roll of the names of able-bodied males in the Town Hall. The militia was a 'home guard' kept in training in the event of a foreign invasion and Bakewell was a central assembly and drilling point in the Peak.

In an age when newspapers were scarce and the ability to read them minimal, the constable could ask a town crier to make announcements in the streets or the vicar from the pulpit. This last approach gave him access to the town's famous peal of bells and these were rung with great vigour, to the eventual dilapidation of the church tower. Thus the bells were rung for the arrival of George I from Hanover and for his coronation, for the Duke of Marlborough's serial victories against the French, for the triumphant Peace of Utrecht in 1714 and so on. The people assembled to celebrate; bonfires were lit and fireworks were discharged. The constable who set these celebrations in motion was often left to deal with the aftermath of drunkenness and occasional violence. Scenes like these contrast markedly with that portrayed in William Archer's fanciful poem.

A contrast is also made between the surrounding countryside and the town by one John Lowe, writing with hyperbole in the *Royal Magazine* in 1765:

The environs of this town are without doubt the most beautiful and fertile of any in these parts; and, when viewed from the tower of the church, exhibit a very romantic landscape. To the east appears a mountain, extending itself on a long chain to the village of Rowsley, about three miles below Bakewell. The perpendicular height of this mountain cannot be less than a mile; the ascent is very steep, troublesome, and fatiguing, and would be still more so, were it not facilitated by a road which climbs the craggy height in a winding direction, and, having gained the top, is joined by the coach road leading to Chatsworth. The latter road takes a large sweep, and mounts the acclivity of this eminence slantwise, in order to render the passage up and down more commodious and easy for carriages. The whole mountain is very sterile and barren, except in some places, where a few briers and small shrubs decorate the surface. On its sides are several quarries of good free stone; and from its summit a delightful prospect of the town below, the beautiful windings of the river, the fertile meadows, hills, vales, woods, and, in short, of the neighbouring towns and villages for several miles distant.

But to return to Bakewell: the whole (a few houses excepted) exhibits a very wretched appearance;

Left: *Gritstone signpost cut in Bakewell c.1709 and originally sited between Edensor and Bakewell. A hand points the way to Chesterfield.*

consisting, for the most part, of low, smoaky, mean edifices: the streets are very dirty, particularly the principal, where, to increase the narrowness, which is very considerable, a whole group of shoemakers-shops, cobblers-bulks, etc. are erected on both sides, and present a rude medly of joysts, rafters, and beams, whose craggy projections, by thrusting themselves into the street, incommode the passengers, destroy the vistoe, and at the same time fill a traveller with fears, less these ponderous fabrics should tumble about his ears, and bury him in their ruins.

In the principal street is a good inn, in the yard of which a large, but cold, spring arises; had it been hot, it would doubtless have been converted into a bath, which would have been attended with considerable advantages, both to the town and inn itself. The other springs in this town are almost of the same spawish quality with the bath-spring; the hot and cold springs are numerous, and conveyed by the drains, under ground, into the river; so that several parts of this town, if one may believe the inhabitants, are almost wholly excavated.

The number of houses cannot be readily ascertained; few are deserving of the name of a house, so that we must not hastily apply the term to the buildings, though they are most of them inhabited; but the whole promiscuous group of messuages, cottages and tenements, may amount to about 260. The sessions for the peace for the northern parts of this county are held in a structure not grand, but commodious. Here is also 4 good fairs held annually; but its market, which is on Mondays, is so mean, that it does not deserve to be mentioned.

Working closely with the churchwardens, the Parish Vestry and the parish constable were the overseers of the poor. Their duties were to distribute parish relief to the genuinely destitute, to deal with illegal 'foreign' immigrants, that is, those belonging to another parish, and to deport any other spongers or tricksters. Thus in 1679 they spent 1s.10d. (9p) in 'removing ye dancing master' from Bakewell. By the 1601 Act residents in the parish had to have certificates to prove they were born there or had right of settlement and from time to time checks were made, followed by expulsions.

The fathers of bastard children or those who had deserted their family were pursued with vigour in order to ensure that they paid regular maintenance and that the cost did not therefore fall on the parish. Errant fathers did not escape, whatever their standing in the community. In 1800, for instance, the overseers had:

The Duke of Rutland's estate map of Bakewell, 1799. Notice the shape of the islands below the bridge. The clutter of shops and houses in Bridge Street was cleared to create the Square in front of the new Rutland Arms in 1804.

... directions to proceed against Mr Humphrey Winchester to recover arrears that is due to the Town for a Bastard child born on the body of Mary Warhurst there being more than 2 years behind at 1s.6d. (7p) per week.

Winchester lived at Holme Hall and was a wealthy lead merchant. Mary was probably an ex-servant.

A number of old parish charities were at the disposal of the overseers. Widow Broomhead and Staniforth's Charity allowed for ten poor widows to receive one shilling (5p) each November and Gisbourne's Charity, from 1826, provided for 'coarse Yorkshire cloth and flannel' up to £5 in value to be divided amongst the poor. Robert Bott's Charity, as laid down in his will (1665), provided in perpetuity for 7s. (35p) a year to be divided among 'as many poor people as the Minister and Churchwardens for the time being shall think fit'.

The charitable bequest by William Archer of Holme Hall disbursed oatmeal to the poor of the parish. Dr Johnson, in his *Dictionary*, might well employ sarcasm in defining oats as a cereal eaten in England by the horses and in Scotland by the people, but many of the poor in the north of England also relied on oatmeal to provide them with bread, porridge and oat cakes.

Quarries and Mines, Machines and Factories

The 60 years before the accession of Queen Victoria saw the greatest changes yet in Bakewell's history. A miniature industrial and agricultural revolution took place, changing it forever from a market town relying chiefly on a farming economy.

The old local industry of lead mining had passed its peak and the new minerals – 'marble' and chert – became more important in the town. The use of blackstone or black marble – not a true marble but a hard, compacted, bituminous limestone – had attracted pre-Roman settlers. In Elizabethan times Bess of Hardwick had promoted work in the quarries at Ashford to adorn her houses at Chatsworth and Hardwick with marble fireplaces and panelling. One of her craftsmen, Thomas Accres, created an 'ingenious machine' on the Wye at Ashford to cut and polish the marble, much of which was also used on church monuments.

It was Henry Watson (1714–86) of Ashford and Bakewell, son of Samuel Watson, the renowned carver at Chatsworth, who established the marble industry at Ashford and Bakewell. In 1752 he purchased the workshops at Ashford from the widow of John Thorpe of Bakewell. There, beside the Wye on the outskirts of Ashford village, he set up a small factory using water-power to drive his machinery, patented in 1751. This could cut, saw and polish marble as well as turn columns and vases on

The ingenious Watsons. Silhouettes by White Watson of his father, Samuel (top right), *his uncle Henry* (top left) *and himself.*

Great Exhibition medal awarded to John Lomas, 1851, for his exhibit of a black marble fireplace inlaid with coloured marbles.

lathes. The last operation was extended to fluorspar and especially to the newly discovered Blue John from Castleton. Henry Watson's 'machine' was one of the minor wonders of the early industrial revolution and attracted spies and 'tourists' from around the country and abroad. Two of the principal manufacturers of the time, Matthew Boulton of the Soho Works, Birmingham, and Staffordshire potter Josiah Wedgwood, were particularly interested in the marble and spar products from Ashford.

The working of marble and spars spread to Buxton, Castleton, Matlock and Derby and Henry Watson introduced the turning of vases on lathes to

The only known illustration of Sir Richard Arkwright's Lumford Mill before its destruction by fire in 1868.
(PENCIL DRAWING BY JOHN PRICE HALTON, FRCS, 1827)

Arkwright Square. Factory housing at Milford, originally for workers at Arkwright's cotton mill. Note the factory-style windows.

Bakewell. John Lomas of Ashford and Bakewell took over as early as 1806 at his new marble works in Grammer Croft below Bakewell bridge and by 1833 he was employing 12 men to operate his water-powered machinery.

Josiah Wedgwood's interest in the minerals of the Peak extended beyond Blue John and Ashford marble. Embedded in the limestone strata were seams and nodules of the hard siliceous rock called chert, which was particularly common in and around Bakewell. In 1772 Wedgwood had discovered that flint ground between chert stones gave a far superior body to his pottery. He wrote: 'A revolution is certainly at hand… It whitens the body exceedingly more even than flint ground with flint would do.'

Eventually a dozen or so chert mines and quarries were opened in Bakewell over the next 200 years. The most important of these was at Holme Bank

behind Holme Hall. By 1780 between 400 and 500 tons were raised at 8s. (40p) per ton. As 'lord of the soil' the Duke of Rutland took 5s. and the men had the rest. Nevertheless, chert mining was an important part of Bakewell's economy until the 1960s. As the road networks and their surfaces continued to improve, so tons of chert were taken into Staffordshire. Cheddleton Mill, near Leek, which still survives, was one of the main recipients, the chert being used to grind flint, which was then sent by canal for use in the nearby Potteries.

Further employment for men, women and especially children came in the shape of Sir Richard Arkwright's cotton-spinning mill erected on the Wye at Lumford in 1778. This was his second water-powered spinning factory, following the success of his first (1771) at Cromford. Additional housing was essential for his enterprise and in Bakewell he built

Carnival Day, c.1935, at the Arkwright housing in New Street, built for workers at the cotton mill.

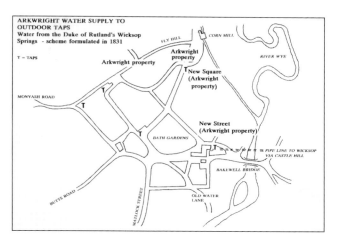

Arkwright water-supply.

The conduit head or water house, Castle Hill House, 1831. It marks the first public water-supply from the Duke of Rutland's reservoir on the edge of Manners Wood. Originally supplying Castle Hill House and Castle Street, it was extended by Richard Arkwright.

cottages including the terraces of New Street and the charming development known as Arkwright Square, with its cast-iron grid windows based on those of his factories. In 1777 a lease was taken on the old parsonage house of the Gells, which was partitioned into tenements for mill workers and eventually purchased in 1796. Across the road from the corn mill Richard Arkwright junior built the Commercial Inn in 1827 to accommodate business associates, whilst over Lumford bridge he lived in the manager's house, once known as Rock House and now Lumford House.

The Arkwrights, like other mill owners, were particularly wary about strangers viewing their premises – especially their machinery. Henry Watson had already experienced industrial espionage at his Ashford marble works and the Arkwrights scrupulously guarded their mills. When John Byng, later Viscount Torrington, stayed in Bakewell in 1790, he walked to the mill and tried to gain entrance. 'But', he tells us, 'entrance was denied for this (no doubt right) reason,

however odd, "That I should disturb the girls"!'

However, all the activities in the mill could not remain secret, especially where the treatment of child workers was concerned. *The Manchester Mercury* reported in October 1786 a shocking case of child cruelty by George Harrison, a worker at the Bakewell mill. He was sentenced at Chesterfield Quarter Sessions to six months' imprisonment and fined £20 for having 'kicked and otherwise abused' a child worker 'in a very unmerciful manner and afterwards drew it up by the neck with a cord. The child was brought in Court and appeared a shocking spectacle.'

However, the Arkwrights looked after their workers in Bakewell better than their rivals in Manchester and elsewhere. Government inspectors said of the mill in 1803, 'Everything in great order' but were more critical later. Here is the report following a medical examination in 1833:

Temperature – Seventy-five.
Ventilation – Moderately good.
Cleanliness – Indifferent.
Work – Begins at 6 o'clock and ends at 7 o'clock.
Relaxation for meals – Half an hour for breakfast, half an hour for tea, and one hour for dinner.
Hot water – Gratis.
Holidays in the year – Christmas day, two days & a half at Whitsuntide; about ten days in the year.
Medical assistance – [Management] subscribes to dispensary and pays accidents.
Total number of persons employed of all ages – About 150 and 200 fluctuating.
Appearance [of mill] – Moderately good.
Situation – Low.
Total number of females under 18 – 46.
    Good health – 18.
    Middling health – 19.
    Bad health – 9.

The doctor added:

Bronchocele [Derbyshire neck] is a very common disease at Bakewell, Matlock and Cressbrook Dale. I saw numerous examples of it amongst the factory children of those places.

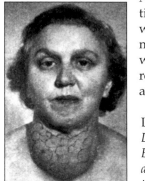

Nevertheless, some rudimentary education was provided for the children, who were generally not taken into employment until their tenth birthday. Schooling was given to enable them to pass a reading test at ten and the adolescents attended Sunday school.

Left: Multi-nodular bronchocele, or Derbyshire neck. Dr Thomas Fentem of Bakewell in 1910 ascribed the curing of this ailment among the young people of the town to the closure of the town wells.

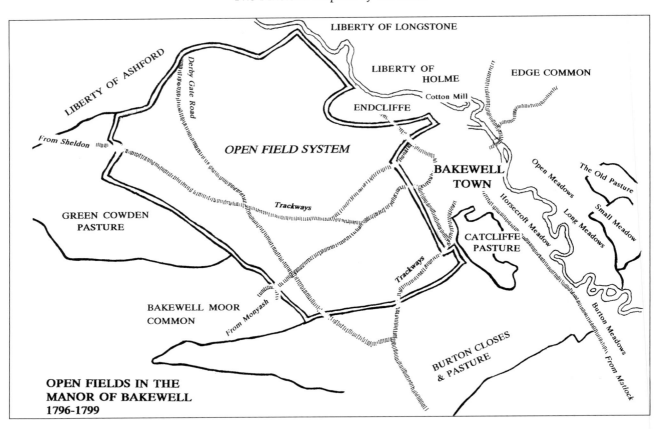

LIBERTY OF LONGSTONE

LIBERTY OF ASHFORD

LIBERTY OF HOLME

EDGE COMMON

Derby Gate Road

Cotton Mill

ENDCLIFFE

From Sheldon

OPEN FIELD SYSTEM

BAKEWELL TOWN

Open Meadows

The Old Pasture

Trackways

Horsecroft Meadow

Long Meadows

Small Meadow

GREEN COWDEN PASTURE

CATCLIFFE PASTURE

BAKEWELL MOOR COMMON

From Monyash

Trackways

Burton Meadows

From Matlock

BURTON CLOSES & PASTURE

OPEN FIELDS IN THE MANOR OF BAKEWELL 1796-1799

The open fields just before enclosure.

Building Arkwright's five-storey cotton mill, together with numerous late-Georgian buildings in the town, increased the need for good stone as opposed to the rubble limestone which characterised much of the old town. The number of quarrymen increased as good ashlar was taken from Bakewell Edge at Wicksop Wood and Ball Cross. This fine stone had been used to build Bakewell church, Chatsworth House and the Crescent at Buxton. The early geologists, John Farey and White Watson of Bakewell, described the stone as 'shale grit' and the latter said it was of:

... a light straw colour... in which are disseminated minute grains of quartz and mica, and concentric ferruginous circles of shaded brown... which have a beautiful effect in ornamental buildings.

It certainly changed the face of Bakewell but, sadly, much of it has decayed and the quarries were worked out by about 1865.

The Enclosure of the Fields in Bakewell and Over Haddon

If industry changed the face of Bakewell town in the late-eighteenth century then improvements in agriculture were to change the surrounding landscape. Small pockets of field enclosure had taken place over the years but the manor of Bakewell still operated the open field system at the end of the century. To some degree this may be explained by the conservatism of an absentee lord, but the system had to change. A series of poor harvests, a prolonged war with France and a growing population were putting great pressure on the open field system nationwide. In the Peak an over-dependence on oats, the poor man's cereal, has still left its legacy in the number of shops and stalls in Bakewell selling oatcakes today.

The old strip system certainly had a bizarre, even picturesque effect, as the German tourist, Carl Phillip Moritz, commented when he walked through Bakewell in 1782:

This field, as if it had been in Germany, was not enclosed with hedges, but every spot in it was uninterruptedly diversified by all kinds of crops and growths of different green and yellow colours which gave a most pleasing effect.

However, the system was wasteful and the Duke of Rutland made a survey in 1799 preparatory to seeking an Act of Parliament which would enclose the land and convert most of it from arable to pasture. This caused huge anxiety in the town as the rights and customs of 1,000 years governing common land were to be changed for ever. The parliamentary commissioners for enclosure appointed William Gauntley as the land surveyor. Thomas and John Barker were nominated as bankers to whom, in 1807, the Duke of Rutland advanced £1,500 for all Gauntley's expenses. The survey began and on 1 March 1808 all rights of commons on unenclosed land ceased and all those claiming rights were assessed.

The arable land was reckoned at 158 acres in the following five fields:

Moorhall field	47 acres
Stanage field	44 acres
Middle field	35 acres
Far field	26 acres
Swindale field	6 acres

The grazing in the pastures, meadows and commons amounted to almost 2,000 acres. Naturally, the Duke of Rutland owned the fields and controlled half the 200 rights of pasturage. Those tenants who had farmed a few strips which were insufficient to constitute a newly enclosed field were often bought out by those with larger holdings. Similarly, some sold their grazing rights. The principal beneficiary in all this swopping and trading was, of course, the duke. In almost all cases he owned the cottages, barns and stables, for which the tenants continued to pay rent.

The old strips, whose contours can still be seen in parts of the fields, were ploughed over and surrounded by limestone walls. Many of these new fields were given over to the grazing of sheep and of young cattle for fattening. As a result, the numbers in the town employed directly or partially in agriculture declined.

The theories of some prominent social and economic historians about the hardship and often penury which Enclosure Acts visited upon the agricultural labouring classes of England do not wholly apply to Bakewell. Few were compelled to leave the town in search of work since the local cotton mills, quarries and chert mines absorbed many who would have been unemployed in areas more dependent on agriculture. Those who had pursued other occupations along with farming their smallholdings quite often concentrated on their main work as innkeepers,

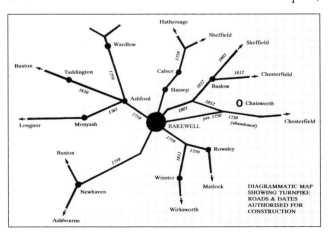

Turnpike roads.

carters, road menders and so on. A few continued work on the land as herdsmen, shepherds and drovers. One of the requirements of the Bakewell Enclosure Act was that the Parish Vestry should appoint a dyke reeve to keep clean the many new dykes and ditches. He employed a small force to carry out the task.

New farms, like Green Cowden, eventually flourished outside the town amid fields now enclosed with dry limestone walls. In the valley bottom, about the town, fields were divided by quickset hedges, fences and ditches. The houses in Bakewell with attached barns for hay and cattle steadily faded from the town's streets.

Farming gradually adjusted and improved, especially at the end of the Napoleonic Wars. The newly formed Scarsdale and High Peak Agricultural Society held its first show in 1819, a modest affair in a field beside the Angel Inn in Chesterfield. The Duke of Devonshire was its first president and in the following year, under the presidency of Sir George Sitwell of Renishaw, it assembled in Bakewell's streets around the newly built Rutland Arms. This was the origin of today's Bakewell Show, once one of the great agricultural shows of the English shires.

The Reorganisation of the Town, 1800–37

The need for better roads and communications in and beyond Bakewell was accentuated by the demands of the new industries in the town, the realignment of some roads in the parish following the Enclosure Act, the growth of the markets and the improvement of transport generally.

New turnpike roads, financed by turnpike trusts and maintained by tolls, began the communications revolution in 1663 on a notoriously bad stretch of the Great North Road. The Peak's first turnpike road, the fiftieth in England, was gradually opened between Buxton and Derby in 1720 as part of the new London to Manchester route. The first such road reached Bakewell from Matlock in 1759 and, gradually, a series of new turnpikes was opened to and from the town. Particularly important was that built by the Duke of Devonshire from his manor at Ashford to Buxton, which improved Bakewell's access to the Peak and Manchester.

Again, the Duke of Rutland, as lord of the manor, had promoted the first turnpike road in 1759 and quickly saw the potential importance of Bakewell as a coaching town and spa. What was needed was a good coaching inn with ample accommodation, good food and extensive stables to replace the White Horse, which satisfied none of these requirements. John Byng, who stayed there twice, in June 1789 and again in 1790, tells us on the first occasion:

I found Bakewell to be a much better place than I

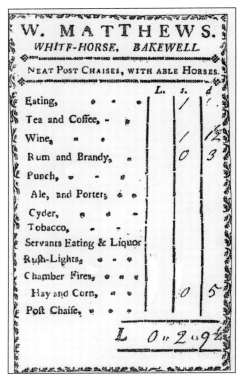
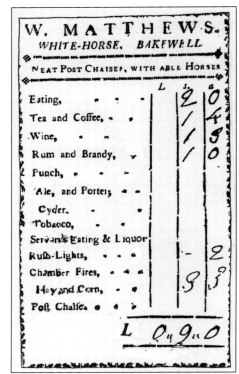

John Byng's bills for his stay at the White Horse Inn, Bakewell, in 1789 (left) *and 1790.*

expected, and the inn, the White Horse, a very good one. The landlady instantly brought before me a quarter of cold lamb, a cold duck, salad, tarts and jellies; and I was eager to enjoy them.

From his bill and his comments beneath one can see how well he ate for a shilling. In the following June he again arrived in Bakewell and lodged overnight at the White Horse. This time he found his stay far from convivial:

Cold ham and cold veal pye for supper. I had no one to speak to... but I will think I was never in a nastier house or a more gloomy place; everything dirty and offensive to the smell... In the night I often arose from my bed to look at the weather; which was very rainy, and continued so till near morning; this was not a place to stay at; I had [i.e. would have] done better at Edensor Inn, only three miles distant. When I got up it was a gloomy black morning, all the hills covered by thick mists; but I was eager to get away; as for master or mistress, they were not to be seen, having, probably, been drunk overnight.

What a contrast! His bill *(above right)* indicates that he ate, or may have been charged, more. However, judging by contemporary remarks by Arthur Young and other travellers he would not in fact have fared any better at Edensor Inn on the Chatsworth estate.

The White Horse Inn could hardly cope with the increasing number of visitors to Bakewell. Set back in the market place in comparison with the Rutland Arms and with an entrance into the butter and corn markets (now King Street), its cramped stables and coach yard backed on to the pig market, so perhaps this location was responsible for the offensive odour to which Byng refers. Part of the stables still survives at the foot of North Church Street.

As owner of the inn, the Duke of Rutland had considered demolishing it as early as 1758, no doubt in readiness for the completion of the Matlock turnpike road. On 1 May 1758 the following notice appeared in the *Derby Mercury*:

Whereas part of the White Horse Inn at Bakewell is to be immediately taken down and rebuilt this is to give notice to any sufficient workmen who are willing to undertake to complete the said building that they are desired to give in their proposals in writing on Tuesday the 16th at 3 o'clock at the said Inn. For further particulars apply to Mr John Barker, Steward to his Grace the Duke of Rutland.

Perhaps this indicates a start on the new stables; the inn itself was not taken down until 1804. As for the new turnpike road, it was driven from Rowsley through what had been Haddon Park, crossed Horsecroft Meadow (now the Bakewell recreation-ground) and entered the town along Horsecroft Lane (now Matlock Street). At a stroke this superseded the old road which had passed along the Park on the higher ground and arrived at the old Town Hall by way of the Butts. Clearly a new town centre was needed and the Duke's map of 1799 gives us the last

The Rutland Arms, c.1910. Built in 1804, its later extensions are shown on the right.

Tuscan portico of the Rutland Arms. The ducal achievement was carved by White Watson.

Silhouette by White Watson of Mrs Ann Greaves (1778–1853), proprietress of the Rutland Arms. Whilst she did not invent the famous Bakewell pudding, she, more than anyone, established its association with the town.

view of the old town before it was changed for ever.

The finest coaching stables in the county were completed by 1805. They were double quadrangular in design, linked by an arch, and this time were located across the road from the inn. The Rutland Arms, as it was renamed, was opened in 1805 and immediately made a name as one of the best coaching inns in England. This reputation was largely due to the proprietors, William Greaves and his wife Ann; he organised the stables and the change of horses whilst she arranged the accommodation, the kitchens and the menus.

Bakewell soon rivalled Buxton as the principal coaching town in the Peak. White Watson tells us that in one week in June 1818, 655 coach passengers passed through Bakewell. According to *Pigot's*

47

Directory of 1835, most of the following changed their horses in the Rutland Arms yard on a daily basis:

To LONDON, the Royal Bruce (from Manchester) every afternoon at quarter past four; goes through Matlock Bath, Leicester, Northampton &c. – and the Peveril of the Peak, at the same hour; goes the same route to Leicester, and thence through Kettering, Bedford, &c.

To BIRMINGHAM, the Defiance (from Sheffield), every morning at ten; goes through Matlock Bath, Belper, Derby, Ashby-de-la-Zouch &c.

To BUXTON, the Peak Guide (from Matlock Bath) every morning at ten, during the season.

To MANCHESTER, the Royal Bruce, and the Peveril of the Peak (from London) every day at half-past twelve – the Lord Nelson, and the Lady Nelson (from Nottingham) every forenoon at eleven; all go through Buxton, Stockport, &c. – and the Champion (from Nottingham) calls at the Wheat Sheaf, every day at twelve; goes thro' Chesterfield, Mansfield &c.

To MATLOCK BATH, the Peak Guide (from Buxton) every afternoon at four, during the season.

To NOTTINGHAM, the Lord Nelson, & the Lady Nelson (from Manchester) every day at half-past two; both go through Matlock Bath, Belper, and Derby – & the Champion calls at the Wheat Sheaf, every afternoon at two; goes through Chesterfield, Mansfield, &c.

To SHEFFIELD, the Defiance (from Birmingham) every afternoon at four; goes through Baslow, &c.

Besides passengers, these coaches carried the Royal Mail and Bakewell was one of the main Post Offices in the Peak. The earlier Post Office was lodged in the White Horse, where in 1799 Robert Innes Smith was 'deputy' (deputy, that is, to the Postmaster General, the equivalent of today's postmaster or postmistress).

The Post Office was transferred to the new Rutland Arms in 1805 and William Greaves became the deputy, often assisted by his wife, Ann. The duties were arduous, for the day began with despatches at 4a.m., with the office open for the receipt of mail as late as 10p.m. In winter additional horses were attached to the usual four in order to haul the coaches along the snow-clad hilly roads. A postilion rode one of the pair of lead horses. The Greaves family kept records of these arrangements in a 'Snow Book'.

As if all this was not sufficiently taxing, Mrs Greaves ensured the smooth running of the inn for the coach trade and for tourists passing through the town. It was she who helped to make Bakewell world-famous for its puddings, which were baked at the inn from the early-nineteenth century. The mythology of culinary mistakes made by a kitchen assistant, usually recounted as the origins of the pudding, are (not very) old wives' tales and can be discounted here; so can all the razzamatazz, still current in the town, about secret recipes and secret ingredients. The truth is that the pudding which made Bakewell famous has origins elsewhere, in Tudor or even earlier times.

The first printed recipe for a Bakewell pudding occurs in Margaret Dods's *The Cook and Housewife's*

Times of mail coaches passing through Bakewell on the Derby-Manchester run, August 1840.

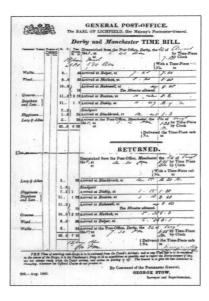

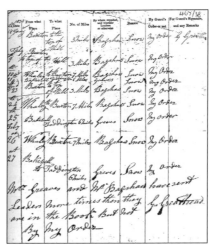

A page from the 'Snow Book' kept by Mr Greathead, mail guard on the Manchester to Derby mail coach, 1830.

Letter from Revd Peter Walthall, curate of Bakewell, to the Bishop of Lichfield and Coventry. This was franked at Bakewell Post Office in 1798.

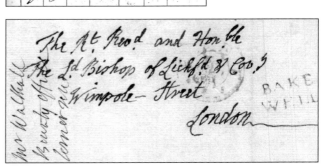

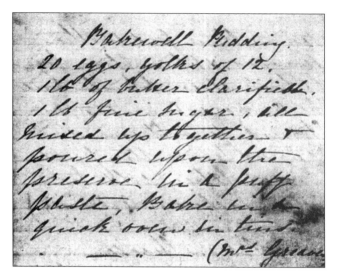

Mrs Greaves's recipe for the Bakewell pudding, copied into the recipe book of Mrs Thornhill about 1863. This is the earliest known manuscript recipe for Bakewell pudding. Notice that neither ground almonds nor almond essence is used.

Manual in 1826, and as late as 1855 Eliza Acton in her *Modern Cookery for Private Families* tells us 'this pudding is famous not only in Derbyshire, but in several of our northern counties, where it is normally served on all holiday occasions.' The earliest known recipe by Mrs Ann Greaves is to be found copied into the recipe book of Mrs Thornhill of Great Longstone in 1863.

So the new Rutland Arms made an immediate impact. Passing travellers included William Wordsworth, who composed sonnets on Chatsworth House and Oaker Hill. J.M.W. Turner also came during a sketching tour of the Peak, when he made a number of drawings of Bakewell and its vicinity. However, despite a century or more of speculation among literary commentators, Jane Austen never came to Bakewell; she never visited Chatsworth or the Peak; *Pride and Prejudice* was neither written nor revised in the Rutland Arms and she never consumed a Bakewell pudding there!

In front of the Rutland Arms the row of old shops running down to Bridge Street and described above by John Lowe in 1765, was cleared away to enlarge the market place (today's Square). By pulling down some old houses and outbuildings across from the inn and alongside the new stables and coaching yard, a walk was opened between the inn and the town's bath. The Duke of Rutland was clearly trying to emulate his neighbour, the 5th Duke of Devonshire, who had revitalised Buxton Spa. The Bath House was extended and leased to White Watson, who continued to live there with his wife following his Uncle Henry's death in 1786. This was fortunate for the town, since Watson was the most talented man living there at the time – a botanist, geologist, sculptor, antiquary and countryman. It was he who laid out the new Bath

White Watson's business card, 1790.

Bath Gardens, originally laid out by White Watson FLS, as a botanical garden after 1805. Today they are planted with an herbaceous border and beds of annuals. The view here looks towards what was originally the Derby Savings Bank (1848), which in 2005 is Lloyds TSB.

Gardens as a botanical garden with two tufa summerhouses lined with mineral specimens and fossils under their thatched roofs. Watson, who was elected a fellow of the Linnaean Society, grew specimen plants in the garden and experimented with methods of propagation. He tells us that in this garden, which is formed of black mould, trees and plants grow very luxuriantly. As for the bath, Watson and his wife opened it as an amenity to visitors to the town and especially to those staying at the inn. In 1817 they advertised the bath as follows:

Ladies and Gentlemen are respectfully informed that the ancient Bath, at Bakewell, having undergone a thorough Repair, is now open for their accommodation.

The Bath is the most spacious in the county, and the temperature of the spring (60 Fahrenheit) renders it admirably calculated for Cold Bathing; the Bath will be emptied every night, and an abundant supply of fresh water will flow to it at all other times.

Mrs Watson at the Bath House has a complete assortment of Linen and Dresses, and she begs to assure those Ladies and Gentlemen who may intend to use the Bath, that every attention shall be paid to their convenience and comfort.

Castle Street, a late-Georgian terrace, c.1815–20.

White Watson, who drank the waters and bathed in them himself, attests to the cures of various patients, of whom the following is an example:

1817: George Hanby of Bolsover recommended by Mr Firth, surgeon. Hepatic and nephritic disease. Restored to his wife and nine children. June 29th, began to bathe every morning until 12th July and drank the water, when he went home on foot cured. Attested to by Mr Firth to Mr White Watson who also saw him in good health in 1823.

However, the Bath House was also an important meeting place for plantsmen, historians, industrialists, scientists and geologists, especially after White Watson had published *The Strata of Derbyshire* in 1811. Such important writers as John Whitehurst and John Farey came; so did Josiah Wedgwood, Matthew Boulton and Erasmus Darwin. They consulted Watson, walked in his garden and viewed the minerals, fossils and artefacts in his museum. Some came to purchase one of Watson's cabinets of minerals or one of his strata of Derbyshire composed of mineral inlays.

The reorganisation of Bakewell's market place and Bath Gardens led to further developments by the Duke of Rutland. The ancient corn mill was rebuilt in a factory style in 1800, no doubt influenced by Lumford Mill. A tasteful Regency terrace (Rutland Terrace) was erected at the beginning of Mill Street (Buxton Road); large houses were rising at the end of Bridge Street, as was the elegant new Castle Street. Shops and houses sprang up along Horsecraft Lane (Matlock Street). The town was rapidly being Georgianised.

The general appearance of the streets, however, was not helped by the cattle markets that continued to be held there. Visitors commented on the dirt and smelliness of the town and coaches found difficulty in passing through droves of animals. In 1826 all livestock sales were removed to a croft adjacent to the Peacock Inn and to Nursecroft, behind the Red

Lion. The other markets for cheese, corn, butter, etc., had already been moved to the area around the old Market Hall. Having cleared the streets it was necessary in 1828 to widen the bridge to allow two-way traffic.

The Rise of the Professional Classes

As aristocratic influence in the town slowly began to decline through the nineteenth century, so the rising professional classes began to exert more control in local affairs. The demise of Gell influence assisted in this process. The baronetcy granted to Sir John Gell in 1642 had died out after three generations and the family's estates and name came by marriage to the Eyres of Holme Hall. In 1796 the Gell estate in Bakewell, which in 1777 was largely leased to Sir Richard Arkwright, was auctioned at Matlock Bath. Arkwright bought up the leases and established his son, Richard, in Lumford House as manager of the mill.

Finer houses than this were being erected in and around the town. Castle Hill House, with considerable grounds extending from Bakewell bridge to Ball Cross and along the Baslow Road, was built in 1785 by Alexander Bossley. He was an attorney and son of William, a well-to-do mercer in the town. Alexander died unmarried in 1826, aged 79, and his house passed to his cousin, John Barker, a wealthy lead merchant who already owned Bagshaw Hall.

The Barkers succeeded the Bagshaws as the Duke of Rutland's stewards in the eighteenth century. Some branches of the family became lawyers and built the fine residences of Burre House and Brooklands. In the town, too, other lawyers' houses graced the street scene – the Denmans' fine early-Georgian house in Bridge Street, now partially screened by later shops, and the mid-Georgian house of the Mander family in King Street.

In King Street, too, the first professional banker established his business. Remarkably, Bakewell still possesses four banks, but James Taylor's premises, though no longer a banking house, were the earliest. Born at Retford in 1788 the son of a book seller, James came to Bakewell as a mercer and built a large house in King Street opposite his small banking office alongside the Rutland Arms.

The apothecaries of the sixteenth and seventeenth centuries were gradually joined by physicians, doctors and surgeons, some of whom had had a university education or medical experience in the Armed Forces. This new professionalism is well illustrated by the monument in the Parish Church to John Denman of Bridge Street, 'a very able and honest apothecary of this town,' who died 25 September 1752. John's epitaph also tells us of his two sons, born in Bakewell:

Joseph became an eminent physician and was for many

Castle Hill House, c.1910, originally built by Alexander Bossley in 1785.

Bridge House, early-nineteenth century. The tufa work in the gardens, said to be by Sir Joseph Paxton, may be by White Watson, who did similar work in Bath Gardens.

years an active and intelligent magistrate in this neighbourhood; Thomas, a physician in London, caused this tablet to be erected in the year 1815.

Thomas was a court obstetrician of distinction; his son became Lord Chief Justice of England in 1832.

It was, however, King Street, not Bridge Street, that became the medical centre of the town in the nineteenth century. We do not know the apothecary who, in 1780, built the façade of a new shop on the street front of a sixteenth-century house at the edge of the butter market. This still survives, as does the remains of the coach arch into Mander's stables next door. The double bow-windowed shop may once have carried the traditional sign of a mortar and pestle. It remained a chemist's shop until 1953, when Mrs Thomson sold the shop and the courtyard to the rear to Maurice Goldstone, an antique dealer.

Aldern House, built in 1825, now extended as the headquarters of the Peak District National Park Authority.

Almost adjacent, at the junction of Church Alley and North Church Street, was built what became known as the Doctor's House. In 1780 the property was conveyed to Edward Buxton of Bakewell, surgeon and apothecary. The house then passed to Charles Farnsworth of the same profession, then to his son and so to subsequent medical practitioners until the death of Dr John Emerson in 1992.

The third part of the 'medical triangle' was the old St John's Hospital. Whilst not a hospital in the modern sense of the word, it did dispense medical care to its six elderly inmates. However, as the town expanded, so did the number of poor and sick who could not afford medical attention; something giving wider benefits was needed.

Philanthropic help came in the form of the Bakewell Dispensary, which was set up by public subscription in 1828. At first it opened in Mill Street (Buxton Road) and was still there in 1835, according to *Pigot's Directory*. A year or so later it was moved next door to the apothecary's shop in King Street, of which the proprietor was Thomas Mills, newly arrived from Sunderland. As one of the officers administering the dispensary on behalf of the trustees, he was assisted by Joseph Harris, surgeon, of Bridge Street and Daniel Reed, physician in ordinary, of Church Lane.

These professional men of various callings, with their families, contributed to the new social and recreational gatherings in the town. Not all of these were successful; for instance, travelling theatre companies occasionally performed in barns, the Rutland Arms or the old Town Hall, but Bakewell never boasted a purpose-built theatre. Similarly, although horse racing was recorded on Bakewell Moor as early as 1749, a regular meeting and a proper course never materialised.

Card clubs such as that of the Revd Peter Walthall in South Church Street were demure, middle-class affairs. White Watson tells us of an oyster club and a short-lived Derbyshire Natural History Society founded in 1799. The professional and business communities led quiet lives; very often they were out of Bakewell about their affairs. To experience a riot in

Milford House. The Georgian house was purchased about 1876 by Robert Cross, a retired cotton manufacturer from Blackburn. He added the Victorian wing.

Burre House in Holme Lane, built by John Barker c.1820.

Brooklands House, another Barker house, built in the late-eighteenth century.

Catcliffe House, King Street, c.1750, built for the Mander family, solicitors in the town.

Thompson's pharmacy, c.1895.

their quiet market town was unheard of. Yet in 1797 this is exactly what happened.

Britain had been at war with revolutionary France for four years. The parish constable had summoned those men of the parish who were eligible for service in the local militia or who might be pressed to enlist with the regulars. Tensions had been high throughout the land at the local musters; there was general resistance to any possibility of being called on to serve abroad. In Bakewell, as the constable began to conduct a ballot of those who were prepared to pay substitutes to do service in their stead, the men would hear no more. They pushed the constable aside, stormed up the steps into the courtroom of the old Town Hall, removed the Militia Roll recording their names and ages and ceremoniously burnt it outside in the butter market.

The JPs were informed and they in turn reported to the lord lieutenant of the county. He summoned the Roxburgh Fencibles, a county militia composed chiefly of regulars, which was in the vicinity. Order was restored and, as punishment, Bakewell lost its Quarter Sessions, which were transferred from the old Town Hall to Derby. There were no further riots and Bakewell settled down again. Indeed, as the French threat increased and Napoleon prepared to

Bakewell Dispensary. This building reveals the filled-in arch of John Mander's coach-house for Catcliffe House opposite. The dispensary was upstairs in the room to the right, next door to the chemist's shop.

Late-seventeenth-century ruined cottage in Church Lane, below Cunningham Place, where tradition has it that John Wesley preached.

invade in 1805, many loyal townsmen and parishioners not only joined the militia but enlisted as regulars. They saw service in the Peninsular campaigns and were present at Waterloo in 1815.

Churches New and Old

White Watson, commenting on late-Georgian Bakewell, tells us that 'on Sundays all went to church, all prayed to one God and the Lord Jesus Christ, and drank in the social parties.' On the face of it this statement seems to reiterate the idealism of John Archer a hundred years earlier. If by 'church' Watson means All Saints' Parish Church, then he is not strictly accurate. A variety of new denominations was gradually taking root in Bakewell.

The terms 'independent', 'Dissenter' and 'Nonconformist' were used from the late-sixteenth century to describe any groups or sects who would not conform to the Prayer Book, doctrine and liturgy of the Church of England. Initially these terms included the Roman Catholics, though by the time of the Civil War the terms were only applied to Protestant sects. Catholics were generally referred to as recusants or, more pejoratively, as Papists. The Toleration Act of 1689, following the Glorious Revolution, gave some concessions 'to their Majesties' Protestant subjects dissenting from the Church of England from the penalty of certain laws.' Henceforth freedom of worship was permitted providing Dissenters took a simple oath of allegiance to the Crown. Strangely, despite these relaxed conditions, Dissenters, who at the time accounted for some five per cent of England's population, declined in numbers for the next half century and then rose quite markedly.

We can trace their early increase in Bakewell to 1788, when a Mrs Noton of nearby Birchills was instrumental in gathering together a group of Dissenters in Bakewell and inviting itinerant preachers to conduct meetings. They met in barns, but the lack of a resident preacher in the town meant meetings were sporadic. They became known as Congregationalists or, in Bakewell at least, as 'Congos'. Their numbers, if not their organisation, increased in the town and parish and they invited students from the Rotherham Academy to preach. By 1804 they had erected a small chapel in Mill Street (Buxton Road). This was extended in 1824 to provide seating for 400 worshippers and a Sunday school for 160 children.

The Methodists were a new sect which outgrew the others by the early-nineteenth century. Their founder, John Wesley, was visiting in the Peak in 1788 and tradition has it that he preached in Bakewell at a cottage in Church Lane where now stands an electricity sub-station. However, Methodism had its followers in Bakewell some ten years earlier and Samuel Smith, a breeches maker, is said to have been the first Methodist in the town. The new and growing sect started a Sunday school in 1778, 12 years before that of the Church of England. By the end of the Georgian period the Methodists had the largest congregation after the Church of England, drawing away numbers from the 'Congos'. Early Methodist meetings were held in private houses until, in 1799, a chapel was built on the site of today's London House, opposite the present Methodist Chapel.

The Quakers, the smallest of the sects, are said to have acquired their name in Derby when, in 1650, Justice Gervase Bennet, having been advised by George Fox, who was brought before him, to tremble at the word of the Lord, dubbed Fox and his followers 'Quakers'. They made little impact on Bakewell until the mid-nineteenth century, though they were present in the parish as early as 1700. In that year Cornelius Bowden of One Ash Grange, a farm near Monyash, obtained a licence to hold meetings there.

The most penalised of all the Dissenters were the Roman Catholics who, before the Reformation, had been the established church in England. Memories of Mary Tudor, the Gunpowder Plot, the reign of James II and the subsequent Jacobite rebellions did not

All Saints' Parish Church with its spire removed, 1820.
(DRAWING BY JOHN PRICE HALTON FRCS, 1831)

*The neo-classical Roman Catholic church at Hassop, 1818.
The design was exhibited at the Royal Academy in 1819 by
the architect, Joseph Ireland.*

Bakewell church without its belfry and spire.
(LITHOGRAPH BY DOUGLAS MORRISON, 1840)

endear them to a Protestant nation of which, in about 1750, they numbered some two per cent. However, following the defeat in 1746 of the Young Pretender, Charles Edward Stuart, and the subsequent growth of toleration in the late-eighteenth century they began to increase, especially in the cities. In rural Bakewell they were few in number and they looked to the old Catholic Eyre family of Hassop Hall for local leadership. Francis Eyre inherited the title of 6th Earl of Newburgh in 1814 and in 1816 erected for his fellow Catholics in the area a most interesting church in the form of a graeco-etruscan temple dedicated, like the Anglican Parish Church, to All Saints. Catholics from Bakewell walked or rode the two miles to Hassop to attend Mass.

As for Bakewell's All Saints, it attracted the largest congregations. Its brand of Anglicanism, then as now, was 'broad' rather than 'low' and, as a comfortable living with some prestige in the diocese of Lichfield, it was well served by capable clergy. Yet the Parish Church was facing a crisis both administrative and economic. On the one hand the size of the parish was shrinking along with its income. The chapels of ease, as we have seen, had been involved in disputes with the mother church over the centuries and matters were coming to a head at the beginning of the nineteenth century. The graveyard which the chapels were obliged to help maintain had little remaining space for burials. The nine chapels began to use their own burial grounds and resented being asked to make contributions towards the decayed fabric of the Parish Church.

The church building had been increasingly neglected since the Reformation, more especially the whole structure of the tower, bell-chamber and spire. The southern arch of the crossing tower where it leads into the Newark had begun to buckle and, although it had been crudely shored up with

unsightly timber props, the pressure from the steeple above was pushing the Newark walls out of perpendicular. Moreover, according to an architect's report in 1817, the cracks appearing at the foot of the spire allowed 'a great quantity of rain and snow into the interior'. Matters did not improve and another architect, writing seven years later, advocated the urgent removal of the spire, octagon and tower to the very foundations and the building of a new steeple and belfry at the west end of the nave.

The whole town was shocked, especially the bell-ringers. A new peal of eight bells, by Thomas Mears of Whitechapel, had been hung in 1797 and a new musical clock, by John Baddeley of Pattingham, near Wolverhampton, had been set in the belfry in 1814. The next year the bells had been rung all day following news of the great victory at Waterloo. The clock played its round of tunes, a different one for each day of the week. Outwardly all had seemed and sounded well.

In 1825 the spire was removed and in 1830 the octagon, including the bells and the clock, was dismantled, the stump of the tower being capped with lead. At the end of a century and a quarter of growing Georgian prosperity, therefore, Bakewell's splendid symbol of ancient settlement and civilisation resembled a dismasted vessel beached above the town.

✦ CHAPTER 5 ✦

Victorian Bakewell

Before the accession of Queen Victoria in 1837 the population of the town had previously, in the census of 1831, been reckoned at 1,898. This represented an eight-fold increase in the 750 years since the compilation of Domesday Book. Pigot described Bakewell parish in 1835 as:

... the most extensive in the county, being more than 20 miles in length from north-west to south-east, and upwards of eight in breadth, containing nine chapels of ease: its population... in 1831 amounted to 9,503.

This figure includes the population of Bakewell township, which continued to rise steadily throughout the Victorian period:

Census	Population	
1841	1,976	
1851	2,217	
1861	2,441	*(+263 temporary workers on the railway and their families)*
1871	2,285	*(boundary changes)*
1881	2,502	
1891	2,748	
1901	2,850	

Compared with neighbouring Buxton and Matlock, however, Bakewell was now outstripped in size.

Few could rival the loyalty shown to the Crown by Bakewellians, though in 1837 they had no church bells to accompany the coronation festivities. Despite this deficiency the pattern of celebration, well established for the recent coronations of George IV and William IV, was repeated. First, prayers for, and proclamations of loyalty to, the young monarch were offered in the town's places of worship. Flags, bunting and fireworks heightened the atmosphere and then the serious business of feasting began.

Between 12.00 and 1.00p.m. a roast dinner was served in a tent in the cattle market to men and youths over 14 years of age. The women, who had served the men, sat down at 4.00p.m., together with the girls over 14, to a meat tea in the same tent. There was a general expectation of peace and prosperity and a sense of impending greatness under the new, young monarch. The town's economic growth in the early part of the queen's reign is well accounted for in the following arguments for routing the proposed Midland Railway through the town on its way from Derby to Buxton and Manchester. The open letter from which the following is taken was addressed to the Honourable G.H. Cavendish, MP for Derbyshire, by L.F. Bingham, landlord of the King's Head Arms (formerly the Crown) in Buxton Road, Bakewell:

Your satellites frequently remind us in terms of bitter

The Butts. A grass-thatched cottage, c.1880. The track beyond used to be called Bear Lane. The late Richard Cockerton remembered gypsies with performing bears passing this way.

The sheepwash at Lumford Bridge, c.1910.

sarcasm, that we do not number 2,000. If so, we shall then have manifest proof that there must be a great influx of persons annually into Bakewell, when I inform you of the immense consumption therein. During the past year there has been slaughtered in and for consumption therein 313 beasts, 1,291 sheep, 186 calves, 256 pigs. We have consumed 194 hogsheads of sugar, 362 boxes of soap, 176 chests of tea, 3,528 sacks of flour, besides some portion of the 16,650 sacks manufactured at Messrs Darwent's mill during the past year; 175 cwt of coffee, 308 cwt of rice, 63½ puncheons of molasses and 830 barrels of ale and porter brought into the town exclusive of Baslow and Litton agencies; and add to these the produce of 415 quarters of malt, brewed by the publicans of Bakewell, and then 184¼ quarters

sold amongst the private families, besides more which I could not correctly ascertain; and then I think you will admit that a large portion is left after our wants have been supplied, and rest assured, little indeed will be wasted.

I must further point out to you the insignificancy of Bakewell, as a village, by informing you that we consume 5,600 tons of coal per annum, 357 hides of leather, independent of any portion of the 1,050 tanned in the place; 462 skins, also clear of the 624 prepared at home; and that amongst other trifles we have had come into the place for the year, 421 bales of goods, 158 tons of black marble; 257 cases, 3,066 parcels, 94 puncheons of wines and spirits, 242 tons of lime, 580 tons of sand, 945 deals, 140 tons of slate, 34 casks of goods, 18 tons

Bakewell cattle market, c.1900. The old Market Hall is in the background.

The Rotherham & Sheffield Bank (1838), now the Royal Bank of Scotland.

11 cwt of iron, 55 boxes of tin, other boxes 190, 16 tons of bones, 147 tons of earthenware, 28 tons of salt, 40½ cwt of white lead, 940 gallons of oil, 105 gallons of turpentine, 169 hampers, 77½ bags of nails 56 lbs each, 2 tons of hemp, 220 tons of paviours, 26 tons of cement, 16 tons of plaster, 1,200 bundles of laths, 44 sacks of linseed, 52 sacks of peas, hewn timber 20.875 cubic feet, 55 crates of glass, 17 tons of sheet lead, 32 dozen spades and shovels, 7½ dozen scythes, 1½ dozen hay knives, 13 bundles of whips, 56 patent bazils; for roller leather at the cotton mill, 1,236 skins; at the same place are received 1,000 bales, or 200 tons of cotton; 106 casks of 6 cwt each and 44 pack sheets are returned, with manufactures.

We have 26 cattle markets yearly, and 5 fairs, on which days are offered for sale 6,700 head of cattle, 8,400 sheep and upwards, with calves and pigs in great

numbers. And although (in evidence given in the House against our title to a Railway) it was stated that 'One Truck' would take all the cheese that came to Bakewell 'in a year… We really cannot believe it, and simply for this reason. On the last five fairs, 259 carts brought 250 tons, besides that made at Bakewell; 200 tons and upwards pass through to Chesterfield, and more than 600 to Sheffield. Rather a large truck load; and, besides this, many hundred tons are brought in the neighbourhood by the factors, all of which would be brought for transit by Railway, in the event of our having one. More than 700 tons of pig lead is carried through Bakewell, and 400 extra tons of coal to the

James Taylor, banker (on the right), reclining in his garden behind King Street, c.1890. The house became a Co-operative store and in 2005 is an antiques centre, with a car park on the croquet lawn. The chimney in the background belonged to the bakery of Gilbert & England, at the corner of Matlock Street.

Taylor's Bank in King Street moved to these purpose-built premises in Water Lane. At the time of writing they belong to the National Westminster Bank.

Alport smelting furnaces, 210 tons of cotton twist, 1,000 tons of caulk, and from it 900 tons of chert.

An increase in banking accompanied this expansion in trade. Taylor's Bank in King Street was joined in 1818 by a bank in Bath Street. Initially known as the High Peak Savings Bank, it later became the Bakewell Savings Bank and later still the Derby Savings Bank (today Lloyds TSB). In 1848 the fine building now standing was erected on the same site. Even more imposing in the old market place (the Square) was the Sheffield and Rotherham Bank, now the Royal Bank of Scotland. The Three Tuns, an old alehouse, was pulled down in 1838 to create the site on the edge of Bath Gardens.

Eventually James Taylor the younger sold his business in King Street to Crompton and Evans Union Bank. By 1890 they had moved into new premises in Water Lane, now the National Westminster Bank. A few years later the Midland Bank moved into premises across the road (now the HSBC Bank in the Square), thus giving the town the four banks it still possesses at the time of writing.

L.F. Bingham's reference to 158 tons of black marble concerns the Ashford black marble discussed in the last chapter. It was cut, polished, turned and

Letter with the new stamps franked at Bakewell Post Office, 20 July 1851.

inlaid at Twigg's mill at Ashford and at Lomas's mill in Bakewell. Articles for use or decoration were very fashionable in homes in the first 50 years of Victoria's reign. Jewellery with coloured marble and malachite inlays on a black ground copied the finer pietra dura produced in Florence. Such sombre brooches, pendants and earrings inlaid with convolvulus, harebells, forget-me-not, Derbyshire pansies and other funereal emblems became fashionable as mementos, more especially after the death of Prince Albert in 1861.

However it was at the Great Exhibition of 1851 that this rural craft reached its zenith. Prize medals were awarded to John Lomas of Bakewell for an inlaid black marble chimney piece and to George Redfearn of Ashford for an inlaid marble table. Prince Albert himself exhibited some inlaid marble slabs by Thomas Woodruff of Bakewell which were also awarded a prize medal. Nevertheless, the vogue for Ashford marble was dying by the 1880s. An exhibition arranged at Matlock Bath to revive the declining trade in 1884 was a failure and the water-powered mills at Ashford and Bakewell had closed by the end of Queen Victoria's reign.

To the visitor viewing the town when Victoria became queen in 1837 all seemed busy and prosperous until the eye was drawn to the wreckage of the once fine Parish Church.

Restoration and New Architecture in the Parish Church

A heated architectural debate took place about the 'restoration' of All Saints' Parish Church. The Dean and Chapter of Lichfield employed two architects in succession to report on the problem of repairing the building. The first, Francis Goodwin, recommended in 1824 the total demolition of the church and its reconstruction with the tower, octagon and spire at the west end. This solution horrified Bakewell's parishioners, antiquarians and ecclesiologists throughout the country and not least the Duke of Rutland, whose ancestors reposed in the Newark. All wanted the church restored as nearly as possible to its old appearance. Goodwin's recommendation to remove the bells and take down the octagonal belfry was accepted and carried out in 1829 by the vicar, Henry Hodgson.

The Dean and Chapter's second consultant was the architect Thomas Johnson who, in 1840, impressed upon the new vicar, Henry Kestell Cornish, the calamitous state of the building. He recommended taking down the four columns of the tower and rebuilding it with a belfry, but not with a spire, which he considered could collapse at some future date. The Norman nave should be stripped out and rebuilt in a lighter Gothic style. The Newark should be demolished and rebuilt, while the surviving exterior walls should be recased in ashlar. Since the old Bakewell quarries at Wicksop Wood and Ball Cross had been virtually worked out, it was recommended that the harder, more expensive, ashlar from Darley Dale should be used.

Again the parishioners were hostile. The vicar, quite prepared to stand up to the Dean and Chapter of Lichfield, consulted a little known architect from Sheffield named William Flockton, who presented a scheme, carefully argued and costed, to give back to the church and the town its former spire. The vicar then convened a meeting in the old Town Hall on Saturday 24 October 1840, at which he gave the following address:

The Town of Bakewell holds so important a situation in the Hundred of the High Peak of Derbyshire, and is so well known to travellers and tourists, that it needs only to be named in order that it may be at once brought to their recollection, with all the beauty and interest of the neighbourhood.

To such visitors the following appeal is made, as well as to all others who have the cause of true religion at heart. It is an appeal on behalf of the Parish Church, which forms so picturesque a feature in the scenery; but which, from its dilapidated and dangerous state, requires that immediate attention should be drawn to it.

For a long period of years the imperfect state of the fabric has given more or less alarm to the inhabitants. Not many years ago the spire and tower, which were highly ornamental, were taken down in consequence of their being in a most shattered condition. The south transept has much declined from the perpendicular, and it now presents a most alarming appearance, both within and without. The inhabitants are therefore most anxious to take such steps as shall secure to them the full blessings of attending Divine service within its walls; while it is also their devout wish to preserve the present fabric, as far as it may be possible so to do. The valuable and excellent specimens of Architecture which it contains, from early Norman downwards, render it most desirable that this should be accomplished, rather than that a style of restoration should be adopted not in character with the present building.

From the opinion of an experienced architect it appears that £5,960 will be required to carry into effect this plan of restoration. In order to raise this sum, subscriptions have been entered into by the inhabitants of Bakewell and the neighbourhood, among whom His Grace the Duke of Rutland has munificently contributed the sum of £1,000, and his Grace the Duke of Devonshire £500, and many others have come forward in a most liberal manner. It is feared, however, that after all a considerable deficiency of means will exist, which has led to this appeal, an appeal to which it is hoped Churchmen and Christians of all denominations will generously respond, by lending their aid towards restoring this consecrated House of God to perfect strength and beauty.

Flockton argued his case with the Dean and Chapter, which eventually conceded that his was the most satisfying and the least expensive option. The Duke of Rutland agreed. Response to the appeal came from well beyond Bakewell parish and the materials removed from the old spire and belfry were auctioned on 19 November 1840, to swell the coffers. The committee appointed to oversee the restoration, under the chairmanship of the vicar, authorised Flockton to undertake the task. He duly appointed George Ellis of Curbar as his mason and Joseph Hill and Thomas Booth, both of Bakewell, as plasterer and joiner respectively. In November 1841, scaffolds were erected and the work of demolishing the Newark, the crossing and the north transept began.

Services were temporarily moved to the old Town Hall, which was now therefore shared with Lady Manners School. Meanwhile, screens were erected to close the east end of the nave and the west end of the chancel so that they could be used to store the many monuments, brasses and inscriptions that had to be dismantled, particularly the most famous ones in the Newark. The churchyard was closed to visitors and George Lancaster, a local man, was contracted to begin the demolition. His workforce of local labourers appeared with a convoy of horses and carts before the Newark. The dismantling of the tombs began and the parts were stored in the nave; then the bodies were disinterred. Flockton himself describes the scene most graphically:

The exhumation was a most interesting operation. The work commenced early in the morning. Perhaps a dozen men were employed in it, some engaged in removing the earth (for it was thought necessary to clear away the whole of the chapel so that nothing should be lost or left by partial excavation). As the works proceeded all was attention and expectation. Now a skeleton stretched at full length from east to west was uncovered and gradually visible, then a relic, after that a leaden coffin and so on during the whole day and so completely was the attention of all parties absorbed in the operations that darkness did not stop them. Large fires were lighted in various parts of the church, torches or candles stuck in the walls or carried in the hands of the workmen to throw light into the excavation. It was an unearthly sight. The appearance after nightfall outside the church was awfully magnificent. The night was very dark. There stood the old church without its roof exhibiting by the light of the fires the terrible havoc the workmen had already made in gutting the interior, taking out the glass lights and a partial destruction of the walls. Through every aperture came the murky blare of the fire and torchlights. Through the south door the workmen were to be seen running to and fro presenting their black profiles between the spectator and the firelight. They looked like spirits from another world, busily engaged in removing the dead... As for the poor old church, it seemed as if it had been slain and the fires kindled for its sacrifice and eagerly endeavouring to devour it.

Flockton's excavations of the old tower foundations were deep and thorough. What a pity that archaeological surveys were not kept. The large variety of decorated stones were simply laid out in the churchyard, along with beams, spars and masonry, easy prey for William Bateman to purloin for his museum at nearby Lomberdale Hall. However, the Duke of Rutland laid the foundation-stone on 16 December 1841; the new tower began to rise and the new transepts were 'stitched' into the nave and chancel. The belfry was successfully erected on the new crossing and the eight bells were hoisted back into

place. Finally the new spire and its weather vane were completed and Flockton was vindicated. The work was a startling piece of early-Victorian conservation, though some new details were introduced and the spire was 16 feet shorter than its famous predecessor.

The Parish Church was not free of upheaval for long. Having viewed the success of Flockton's new work, the church authorities now cast their eyes on the ponderous Norman nave. Its thick, square columns made it difficult for the vicar to be seen or his conduct of the services to be heard. The architect Thomas Johnson, as we have seen, recommended that the nave be rebuilt. In 1852 the Sheffield firm of Weightman & Hadfield, whose recently built church at Matlock Bath had aroused general admiration, was commissioned to rebuild Bakewell's nave in the Gothic style. Again, part of the churchyard had to be closed except for burials, though even these were carried out with great difficulty by the sexton, who could barely excavate more than two or three feet before disturbing the remains of earlier inhumations. The churchyard was full and the chapelries refused to pay the church rates for its maintenance. They were by now conducting their own baptisms, weddings and burials and by the end of the century Bakewell had only Over Haddon remaining as part of its once great parish. As for the township of Bakewell, it desperately needed a cemetery which could provide for other denominations besides the Anglicans.

The churchyard was closed for burials in 1858. On 17 November of that year the Bishop of Lichfield consecrated the north-east part of a new burial ground a quarter of a mile to the south of the Parish Church along what was at the time called Cemetery Road, though its modern name is Yeld Road. This was the Anglican burial ground; further on was the portion allocated to the Dissenters. Both areas had their own small chapels, each with a steeple. These buildings, together with an entrance lodge, were the work of T.D. Barry, a Liverpool architect. The

The Parish Church from South Church Street.

The nave of the church in 1851, as rebuilt by Weightman & Hadfield of Sheffield.

Steel engraving, c.1860, of Bakewell cemetery. The Anglican chapel, in the foreground, was consecrated by the Bishop of Lichfield in 1858.

The seventeenth-century vicarage, c.1860s, with the Revd Kestell Cornish returning from church. This may be a valedictory photograph, taken before he left and a new vicarage was built.

Edward Balston, headmaster of Eton College, 1862–67.

Archdeacon Balston, vicar of Bakewell, 1869–91.

Bakewell writer, Andreas Cokayne, enthused that 'it is tastefully laid out and adorned with shrubs and the walks afford pleasant promenade.' And so it is now, though sadly the place has today achieved national attention as the site of a foul and controversial murder.

Hubert Kestell Cornish, vicar of Bakewell from 1840 to 1860, had been instrumental in the great physical changes to the parish of Bakewell and its church. Highly respected as a devout leader of his flock, he retired from Bakewell in a singular way by exchanging his living for that of Edward Balston at Hitcham, in Buckinghamshire. Balston had occupied the Hitcham living for less than a year following his

resignation as headmaster of Eton College. When he came to Bakewell he was of high church inclinations in a fairly low church parish and was initially held in some awe. However, he and his wife and two curates immersed themselves in the life of the parish and won universal respect and affection. His organising skills impressed the Bishop of Lichfield, who appointed him rural dean and archdeacon of Derby.

Balston's private means and his connections with the architectural fraternity enabled him to provide his church and parish with some notable works. First he completed the final stage of the restoration of All Saints' Parish Church by restoring and beautifying the chancel in 1874. For this project he secured

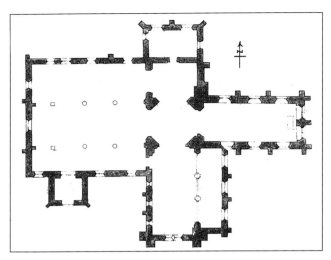

Plan of the Parish Church following the Victorian restorations of Flockton, Weightman & Hadfield and G.G. Scott junr.

Archdeacon Balston's splendid new vicarage, built by Alfred Waterhouse in 1868.

The church chancel after restoration by George Gilbert Scott junr, 1879–82. Note the stencilled walls and the gas lighting.

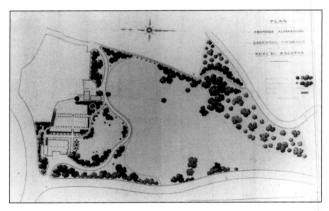

The vicarage grounds (1885) designed by landscape architect Edward Milner, an old boy of Lady Manners School and a pupil of Sir Joseph Paxton at Chatsworth.

the services of his former pupil at Eton, George Gilbert Scott junr. Scott, assisted by Temple Moore, reordered the woodwork in the choir whilst retaining medieval features, erected the high altar with its finely carved reredos and laid an attractive mosaic floor.

As this work started Balston's new vicarage was being completed. The old seventeenth-century vicarage in South Church Street was a conglomeration of small rooms which had grown over two centuries. Balston found it unsuitable, had it pulled down and employed no less than Alfred Waterhouse, architect of Manchester's famous Town Hall, to build him a grand Gothic vicarage with a coach-house. The grounds were beautifully laid out by Edward Milner, a pupil of Lady Manners School, trained by Sir Joseph Paxton at Chatsworth and, at this time, head of a successful landscape gardening practice in London. Balston's new vicarage was like a small bishop's palace and a problem for his successors, who lacked the means to maintain and inhabit it.

His building urge did not stop here. In 1880 the run-down chapel of ease at Over Haddon was removed and H. Cockbain built the pretty church of St Anne with a house for the lay deacon. Archdeacon Balston provided two-thirds of the cost, as he did in his final project, the repair and beautification of the chancel of St Leonard's, Monyash, of which living he was patron. Again a first-rate, high church architect, William Butterfield, was employed.

If Balston brought back much of the prestige of the Anglican church in Bakewell, the other denominations were also flourishing and contributed considerably to the social life of the town with their choirs, Sunday schools, bands and amateur theatricals. Of these the most numerous were the Wesleyan Methodists, who in 1867 moved from their original chapel and put up a new and larger one just across the road whose east end still fronts the street. Behind it was erected a schoolroom and in 1891 a manse for a resident minister. In time for the centenary, a generous bequest enabled extensive modifications to be made to the building and the establishment of a youth club in the cellar of the manse. A further re-ordering took place in 1992 when the opening ceremony of the church as we see it today was performed by Lord Tonypandy, ex-Speaker of the House of Commons.

The movement inspired by John Wesley was to split nationally in 1811, when the Primitive Methodists broke away, and again in 1849, when the Wesleyan Reform movement was born. In Bakewell attempts by the former to establish regular services in a meeting place met with only intermittent success and it took the energy and enthusiasm of a newcomer to Bakewell, Joshua Barrett, to organise them. They rented rooms for this purpose in premises at the top of Bagshaw Hill (Oddfellows Hall) from 1879 until they built their chapel in Water Lane in 1891. The Primitive Methodists amalgamated with the Wesleyan Methodists in the twentieth century and the Water Lane chapel closed for worship in 1944, many members of the congregation joining the Wesleyans on Haddon Road. The chapel is now a newsagents and stationers.

When the Oddfellows Hall was vacated by the Primitive Methodists it was taken over by the Christian Assembly. Meeting originally in the house of a Mr Sellars in The Avenue (off Haddon Road), this group sought to recreate what they considered was a form of worship more in keeping with the New Testament. They used the hall for their Sunday services and, with the continued growth of the Church, bought the whole building in 1949. They renamed it the Gospel Hall and, altering and extending it between 1982 and 1985 by the incorporation of what had originally been stables have, in 2005, completed over a century of worship there.

The Wesleyan Reform established their chapel and schoolroom in 1887. Now a builder and joiner's workshop, it was fitted neatly into the slope of Little Bagshaw Hill, with its main entrance on Buxton Road. This chapel, which in its heyday was much loved and well attended, did not finally close until 1985, when the congregation could not afford the cost of the considerable structural work needed on the fabric. The Methodists in general contributed richly to so many aspects of Bakewell life, particularly in the sphere of education, as will be seen.

Also growing in numbers in the nineteenth century were the 'Congos' (Congregationalists), the oldest dissenting sect, known in the seventeenth century as the Independents. After some years of meeting next door to a public house, they settled their chapel in Mill Street (now Buxton Road) as early as 1804. They enlarged the building in 1824 and 20 years later, as Flockton was tackling the Parish Church, they rebuilt their place of worship in the Gothic style. Soon after the Second World War, when the preacher left Bakewell and was not replaced, the chapel closed, some of the congregation joining the Wesleyan Methodists.

For some years before 1890 Roman Catholic services were held over the stables of the Rutland Arms hotel. Parishioners could choose the stables or a three-mile walk to the elegant classical revival church at Hassop. In 1890 a small church of corrugated iron was built in Granby Road, opposite the police station, subscriptions towards this coming most generously from all the other churches in the town. The 'tin tabernacle' or 'tin tent' was small and simply decorated and, compared with the church at Hassop, was hardly uplifting, but it is remembered affectionately by some of today's older parishioners. When a larger building was needed, the Church bought the former Congregational chapel on Buxton Road in 1948.

Finally, the smallest group, the Quakers, or

Architect's drawing of the Wesleyan Reform chapel, between Bagshaw Hill and Buxton Road. In 2005 this is a builder and joiner's workshop.

An anonymous oil painting of the original house Burton Closes, designed by John Robertson, Sir Joseph Paxton and A.W.N. Pugin. Note Paxton's elegant ridge-and-furrow conservatory.

Burton Closes as extended by T.D. Barry for William Allcard and Smith Taylor-Whitehead.

commercial boarding school kept by the headmaster.' On Kay's death in 1874 Lady Manners Grammar School closed and the income from the endowment was allowed to accumulate under the watchful eyes of R.W. Nesfield, the Duke of Rutland's agent, and the vicar, Archdeacon Balston. The latter extended his benefactions to the town by financing a small grammar school until his death in 1891. As we shall see, Lady Manners Grammar School was not reopened until 1896.

Meanwhile the inadequate provision of schooling in the town prompted various individuals to open a motley array of institutions using small endowments or simply for private profit. The *Directories* euphemistically list them as 'academies' and, whilst none was so deplorable as Dickens's Dotheboys Hall under the monstrous Wackford Squeers, standards were usually very low.

White Watson tells of an early attempt by Mrs R. Pidcock to set up a day school for young ladies in his residence at the Bath House in 1807. The instruction would be:

... in the usual branches of female education on the following terms, viz per quarter, instruction in reading, English grammar, writing and needlework 10/6 [52½p], children under five years of age 7/- [35p], entrance 2/6 [12½p]. Mrs R. Pidcock, having endeavoured to qualify herself for teaching the above branches, ventures to solicit the support of the gentry and inhabitants of Bakewell in her attempt to establish a respectable school in the town.

White's Directory of 1862 listed half a dozen such dame-schools, where young children were taught by unqualified women, usually in their own homes. But then teacher training institutions were only just being established so there was no standard qualification.

Two dame-schools were set up in South Church Street in the 1860s. The first utilised the charitable endowment bequeathed by Mary Hague in her will of 1715. This allowed for seven children to be taught to read the scriptures and was carried out by a succession of women of the old Bakewell family of Bradbury. The second school belonged to Theresa Sousloff, whose curriculum must have appeared as eccentric as her name. One pupil records that the girls studied topics as miscellaneous as sponges, hemp, breadmaking, Edward III, William Tell, the Creation, the Flood and civil, military and naval architecture!

The dames were not necessarily mature ladies who might, like Muriel Spark's Jean Brodie, consider themselves in their prime. Miss Kay, for instance, the daughter of William Kay, headmaster, ran a ladies' boarding school at the age of 16! This was next door to her father's school in Bridge Street and he no doubt kept an eye on her and appointed a governess to assist her. Other dame-schools were those belonging to Jane Wilson and Frances Ditchfield, both in Mill Street, and Miss Terry's establishment in Church Street. Similar schools for boys were run by John Ovens in Rutland Terrace and William Smith in Matlock Street.

The Sunday schools were important in the nineteenth century's progress towards Mass education and gave denominational impetus to the establishment of weekday schools. The Nonconformists, supported by the British and Foreign School Society formed in 1808 by Joseph Lancaster, set up what became known as 'British Schools', which would offer free education for those unable to pay. Joseph Lancaster popularised the monitorial (or Lancasterian) system of teaching which, in his view, was an economic and quick way of disseminating knowledge. The schoolmaster or mistress would teach a class of bright, receptive pupils who in turn would act as monitors and impart the information by rote learning to other children. The Church of England responded with its own 'National Schools', supported by the National Society for Promoting the Education of the Poor. This had been founded in 1811 by Dr Andrew Bell who had also, independently, devised a monitorial method of teaching and learning not dissimilar to Lancaster's.

Bakewell reflected the national picture. By 1833 the Anglican, Methodist and Congregational churches in Bakewell were already teaching and catechising 326 children. In 1848, with aid from the National Society and the backing of the Duke of Rutland, Anglican subscribers opened a National School for Girls. Built at a cost of £680 on land given by the duke at the junction of Little Bagshaw Hill and Rutland Terrace, the school could accommodate 150 children. Attendance was voluntary and some parents paid moderate fees. The girls were taught the 3Rs, religious instruction and needlework and no doubt the monitorial system was employed.

The Wesleyan Reform and Congregationalists responded by opening small schools at their chapels in Mill Street. By 1860 we hear no more of the latter, but in 1867 the Wesleyan Methodists built their new chapel in Matlock Street together with a school for 120 children.

Nationally the pattern of education was patchy and in 1870 the Liberal government passed E.M. Forster's Education Act, which aimed to provide schooling for all children. Non-denominational board schools were to be set up where church provision was inadequate. Bakewell had no need of such a school, but the churches did need to provide more school places for boys. It was decided that a new school should be built for girls and infants and that the premises evacuated by the girls should become the new National Boys School. Once again the Duke of Rutland provided the land for the new building in Bath Street, which was completed in 1872. The Wesleyan school continued in Matlock Street.

This all seemed sound and progressive, but these schools had their failings, as the head teachers' log books and general inspections reveal. Daily education was not yet compulsory and teachers found truancy one of their chief problems. Here are some interesting entries from the log books of the three National Schools.

Infants	Sept 9, 1875	'Children away gathering blackberries'.
	Sept 23, 1875	'A poor school this morning owing in a great measure to a Wild Beast Show in the town'.
Girls	May 22, 1873	'Numbers low. Soldiers passing through the town'.
	Mar 5, 1875	'Only seventeen children were present this afternoon, many of them having to gather firewood which has been given to the poor by Lord George Cavendish'.
Boys	Nov 17, 1874	'Numbers low due to beating in the woods for shooters'.
	June 25, 1875	'Numbers low due to rifle review at Calton'.
	July 9, 1875	'Numbers low due to haymaking'.

Various incentives were tried to improve attendance. On 12 March 1878 we read 'the infants were rewarded with nuts and sweetmeats' and on 31 October 'Archdeacon Balston and his wife distributed books among the boys and pinafores and pocket handkerchiefs among the girls to encourage regular attendance.'

Mundella's Education Act of 1880 helped to resolve the problem by making attendance compulsory for five- to ten-year-olds. Yet activities in the town could still affect attendance. On 31 May 1897, for instance, we read that 'the closing of the cotton mill, chert quarry and scarlet fever in the town have seriously affected the attendance and work of scholars.'

Health and hygiene were constant problems as minor epidemics afflicted the town, some of which emanated from the schools. In 1876 Henry Smith, master of the Boys' School, contracted an illness that was 'directly traceable to the very imperfect sanitary arrangements, the drains being inadequate!' During smallpox and scarlet fever scares the boys' classroom was daily disinfected with carbolic powder for a few weeks and on other occasions 'sprinkled with "Sanitas" four times a day.'

Naturally, against this background the progress of the pupils was not good. A rapid turnover in teaching staff did not help. In 1875 an HMI report on the Boys' School reads:

The state of this school is very unsatisfactory both as to efficiency and numbers. Out of 22 who were examined 14 failed in reading, 6 in writing and spelling, 1 in arithmetic... the unsatisfactory result of the examination is due to want of proper exertion on the part of the master, Mr Gladwin.

The Girls' School was only slightly better. The grants

William Storrs Fox with staff and pupils of St Anselm's School.

to both schools were reduced with threats of further financial penalties if there was no improvement! Both the master and the mistress soon resigned and standards thereafter steadily improved. Better teachers stayed longer, including Mr James Radford, who taught at the Boys' School from 1876 to 1892, and Miss Salt, who served the Girls' School from 1891 to 1927. The Boys' School was closed in 1894 and moved into better accommodation behind the Girls' School in Bath Street.

Private schools enjoyed little success in eighteenth- and nineteenth-century Bakewell until the arrival in the town of a young graduate of Pembroke College, Cambridge, called William Fox, son of the vicar of St John's, Micklegate, York. In 1888 he acquired a site on the northern extremity of the town, at Stanage. His school, which was to become St Anselm's, opened with one pupil in the first term. By term three there were two more.

In 1889 William married Mary Storrs, daughter of Sheffield's town clerk and thereafter he lengthened his name to Storrs Fox. By 1891 he had an infant daughter and a domestic establishment of a nurse,

cook and two servants. There were now 15 boy boarders between the ages of 9 and 13, including Alexander Carrington of Bakewell. Two additional staff were subsequently employed and Storrs Fox held his number at no more than 30 until after the First World War. Thus a steady foundation was established upon which subsequent heads and staff built a sound academic reputation.

The 1860s: Triumph and Disaster

The coming of the railway to the Peak District caused horror and excitement. John Ruskin represented many who loved the beauty of the peaks and dales when he spoke vehemently against its encroachment, just as Wordsworth had done in the Lake District. Businessmen and investors naturally viewed its coming with relish. The people of Bakewell waited anxiously to see which route the Manchester, Buxton, Matlock & Midland Junction Railway would take from Rowsley, which it had reached in 1849. The 6th Duke of Devonshire welcomed the railway, and his gardener and friend Joseph Paxton had shares in the

The collapse of the cut-and-cover tunnel near Haddon Hall during construction of the Midland Railway, 1861.

The Midland Railway Station, c.1920.

company. Paxton built a station at Rowsley to enable the duke and his entourage to move to Devonshire House in London and the duke would have liked a similar station at Baslow to enable him to travel north. This of course would mean that the new line would follow the River Derwent upstream and, obscured from view by a tunnel, would cross Chatsworth Park.

Bakewell canvassed strongly against such a scheme and argued that the line should enter the Wye valley and pass through the town. The Duke of Rutland hesitated and then agreed that it could cross his estate provided that the line was concealed in a cut-and-cover tunnel behind Haddon Hall. The project was held up for the next ten years, during which time the Midland Railway Company took over the line and pondered the formidable engineering problems presented by the hills and dales en route to Buxton. Nor did the rival offers of the two dukes help. Then, in 1858, the 6th Duke of Devonshire died. His successor was opposed to the line passing through Chatsworth Park and the Wye valley route was the only alternative.

The people of Bakewell fondly imagined the new line would follow the River Wye upstream to a station in the town, but the Duke of Rutland would only consider a line out of sight of Haddon Hall. Bakewell Station would thus be situated on the hillside below Ball Cross Woods and half a mile from the town. This scheme being acceptable to Parliament, the line then proceeded to Monsal Dale by a tunnel, spanning the river by a stone viaduct. By tunnels and bridges it passed through Millers Dale and Chee Dale on its way to Buxton and Manchester.

John Ruskin was appalled at the desecration of the dales, especially the ruination of the magnificent view from Monsal Head down into Monsal Dale. In mocking despair he declared:

You might have seen the gods there, morning and evening walking in fair procession on the lawns and to and fro among the pinnacles of the crags, but the valley is gone and the gods with it, and now every fool in Buxton can be in Bakewell in half an hour and every fool at Bakewell in Buxton.

The railway brought considerable benefits of trade and communication to Bakewell and the Peak when the line was opened in 1863. Tourists descended on the town and the Rutland Arms increased its accommodation. The Peak was opened up to that new species of traveller, day-trippers. They could take a carriage from Bakewell and see the sights in quick time, which accounts for the two best-selling guides by Andreas Cokayne of Bakewell, *Bakewell and its Vicinity: Excursions, Drives and Walks* and *A Day in the Peak: Bakewell church, Haddon Hall and Chatsworth*.

The town had barely begun to enjoy the benefits of the Midland Railway when its economy was dealt a serious blow. In 1868 the Lumford cotton mill, which Sir Richard Arkwright had erected barely a century earlier, was gutted by fire. The wooden floors, one above another, a most dangerous feature of early textile mills, were consumed along with their machinery. All but the stone walls was destroyed. The two great water-wheels were left intact, a symbol of the obsolescence of water-power in the face of the safer, steam-powered mills near the Lancashire and

Bakewell cotton mill destroyed by fire, 1868.

The two water-wheels which survived the mill fire.

Yorkshire coalfields. Many people lost their jobs.

The Arkwrights had sold the mill, along with workers' housing, to the Duke of Devonshire in 1860. After the mill burned down Messrs Simpson and Hibbert, who had been lessees since 1844, pulled down the ruinous shell. By 1875 they had restored some reduced textile operations on the site. These were unsuccessful and Bakewell's textile industry concluded with two clothing factories in Buxton Road, the Progress Works in the Arkwrights' old Commercial Inn, and the Melso Works in part of the

Rutland Arms stables. These lingered on into the twentieth century.

Local Government and Social Welfare

The town's prosperity had grown independently of its ability to govern its own affairs. The Municipal Corporations of 1835 were not concerned with unincorporated market towns such as Bakewell. Their administration, like that of some three-quarters of what was rural England, lay in the hands of the local squires, the JPs, many of whom were minor gentry or clergymen, and the Parish Vestries. Slowly, rural areas were accorded measures of self government until County Councils were established in 1888 and Urban District, Rural District and Parish Councils completed the framework of representative local government six years later.

Under the Local Government Act of 1858, Bakewell's ratepayers, at a meeting on 11 March 1863, set up a Local Board which assumed many of the duties in the town and parish previously performed by the Vestry. The old Market Hall in Bridge Street replaced the old Town Hall as the civic centre in 1858. The Justices had been meeting there since Lady Manners School had moved into the old Town Hall's courtroom in 1826. Nesfield converted the old Market Hall into a Town Hall by clearing out the washrooms on the ground floor and creating the courtroom upstairs. Here the new Board met on 12 July 1863, and Robert Nesfield, the Duke of Rutland's agent from Castle Hill House, was elected as the first chairman; ducal influence was still apparent. The rest of the Board consisted of:

James Walters, general practitioner of the Hayes off Matlock Street
James Gratton, bookseller and printer in Matlock Street
Charles Darwent, farmer and miller of Bath Street
James Taylor, banker in King Street
William Greaves, landlord of the Rutland Arms
William Greaves, farmer

Robert Irvine, grocer and wine spirits merchant of the Square
Robert Orme, grocer of the Square.

The new Board appointed the Duke of Rutland's surveyor, Daniel Roberts, as Surveyor and Inspector of Nuisances at a salary of £20 a year, and Ambrose Brookes, attorney, as clerk at the same salary. William Smith junr became the Rate Collector at £6 a year and Edward Pheasey, a tailor of Matlock Street, received 8s. (40p) a week as the town's lamplighter. The first proposed General District Rate was 10d. (4p) in the pound and 2½d. (1p) in the pound for highway maintenance.

The destruction of the mill raised the urgent issue of fire prevention in the town. The mill itself had been equipped with a small four-wheeled pump, similar to those kept in the local country houses. This and a collection of buckets were powerless to deal with the blaze, even though the mill was largely surrounded by water.

A fire brigade with a modern engine was essential, and the new Local Board slowly began to tackle the problem. By 1877 hose-pipes and scaling ladders were purchased and by 1880 a handcart was acquired. In the following year Charles Glossop, a bank clerk, took charge of a volunteer fire brigade for which the Board purchased a new fire engine for £100 in 1884. This carriage, drawn by two horses, was housed in the old butter market beneath the old Town Hall. This 1884 model, from Shand, Mason & Co., served the town until 1912, when a steam-

Bakewell's first fire engine, purchased in 1884 for £100. This hand-pumped machine, driven here by 'Derbyshire Charlie' Hicks, stands outside the new Post Office, c.1895.

Tory Island from Bakewell bridge, c.1890. The marble works are behind the trees on the left and the leat into the water-wheel is beneath the tree.

pumped version was supplied by the Bakewell Urban District Council.

The Local Board's provision of the town's first fire engine in 1884 was associated with the installation of a second and much improved water-supply to the town. The earliest source, piped from Manners Wood, was inadequate for the expanding town and in 1872 the Duke of Rutland agreed to sell for £200 a new supply. This was to be piped from a reservoir on Coombs Hill and a soft-water spring at the Fallinge. Eventually this supplied all the town; the old wells were capped, their pumps and taps were removed and a water rate was set at 1s.3d. (6p). To celebrate this achievement a group of townsmen led by Robert Cross of Milford House erected a water fountain beside the bridge. Today it is still referred to as 'Cross's Folly'. The improvement in public health was appreciable and in 1910 the town's medical

Stone clapper bridge for anglers, Bakewell meadows, c.1900.

J. Waterfall, a disabled resident, outside his almshouse at St John's Hospital, 1890s. Known as the 'Poet of Bakewell', he composed and sold for a penny verses and historical information on local attractions. Some were sent to Queen Victoria.

His cottage interior displayed his writings and a collection of curios for tourists' inspection. Sadly, he was burned to death here.

Church House, with Dr John Knox, his wife Eliza and another lady in the garden, c.1890.

officer, Dr Thomas Fentem, reported that Derbyshire neck, or goitre, was no longer evident in the younger generation.

Yet the principal water source, the river, was being increasingly contaminated by effluent from the villages upstream and from the town itself. The piped water-supply enabled more raw sewage to be flushed into the river, especially from Castle Street. Conversely, when the river was high the drains regularly backed up in New Street, Arkwright Square and

The Square, c.1890. Note the open drain and the 'causeway' to the bank on the left. The jubilee lamp outside the Rutland Arms has one light. Critchlow the butcher (on the left), still advertises 'post horses, phaetons, brakes, waggonettes, governess cars' etc. which were available from the Rutland Arms stables.

The annual fair held in the Square, 1892.

BAKEWELL
URBAN DISTRICT COUNCIL.

Proprietors and Drivers of Hackney Carriages must observe the following Rules :-

1. On and after 24th May, no Carriage will be allowed to take its position on the Stands unless the Number of License granted in respect of such Carriage be painted or marked thereon, in accordance with Bye-law No. 17.

2. Touting for hire is strictly prohibited.

3. Each Driver to stand at his Cab Door while the Train is in the Station, and to keep that place until Passengers have chosen their Cabs.

4. Each Driver to have his Cab on the Stand before the Train is due (Station Time) or to forfeit his place.

BY ORDER.

H. BRAMWELL,

6th May, 1897.   *Manager of Hackney Carriages.*

J. GRATTON, PRINTER, BOOKSELLER, ETC., BAKEWELL.

Hackney carriage regulations, 1897.

Milford. Waste from the cattle and stall markets found its way into the river, whilst the long, open, gritstone drain which crossed the recreation-ground debouched its contents near the point where children swam and paddled in the summer.

An outbreak of typhoid at nearby Bradwell caused general alarm and odd cases in Ashford and Bakewell alerted the medical officer. In 1888 William Smith, the Local Board's Inspector of Nuisances, contracted the disease in the course of his duties. The Board more than once discussed the advisability of some sort of sewage plant, but did nothing. However, a public tip on Ashford Road was provided by the new Urban District Council in 1895.

The town badly needed a hospital. The Dispensary in King Street still operated in conjunction with an inadequate 'lying-in hospital' in Reginald Broomhead's house in Mill Street. Dr John Knox of Church House led the medical practitioners in the town in pressing for a new hospital to mark the Queen's diamond jubilee. Neither this nor the proposed swimming bath to keep people out of the river was achieved. Piped sewage and a filtration plant were not installed until 1937. Meanwhile, the odd case of smallpox caused further anxieties and in 1894, where Lady Manners School now stands in Shutts Lane, a hastily built Infectious Diseases Hospital was erected. This was a wooden structure

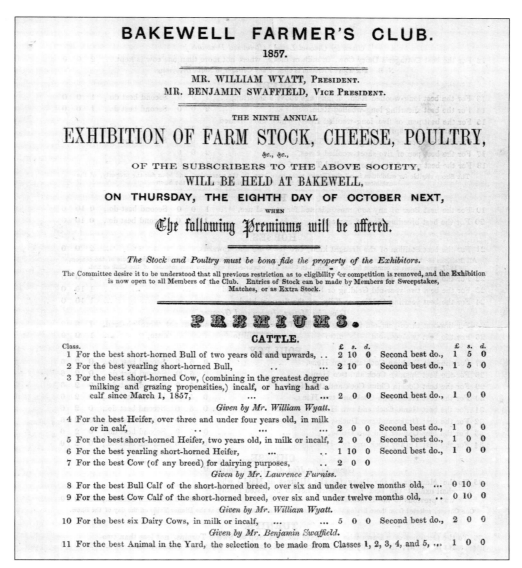

Programme of the ninth annual Exhibition of the Bakewell Farmers' Club, 8 October 1857.

which cost £200 and never housed a smallpox patient. It was later replaced by the Firs Hospital nearby on Monyash Road, though this no longer functions as a hospital.

Bakewell's streets and passages were improving in cleanliness. Horses were still stabled in many yards, but cattle byres were rapidly vanishing and slaughterhouses, especially those adjacent to butchers' shops, were more closely controlled. Few of the streets were metalled, not even the Square, and some banks and shops were approached by causeways. A water cart helped to control the dust in summer, whilst in winter some areas were still churned up. Charles Bradbury tells us how messy the Square could be at the time of the fair. A thick covering of straw was strewn about to absorb the mud and paraffin flares were lit at night to boost the gas lamps.

Gas had come early to Bakewell. By 1850 the Lumford cotton mill had its own gas plant and the streets were being lit by the Bakewell Gas Co. from its works on Buxton Road. The amenity was gradually extended – to the Parish Church and the new Town Hall by the end of the century as well as to houses and shops. The latter reflected the town's increasing prosperity with their grandiose façades and their horse-drawn delivery vehicles operating well beyond the town.

Leisure and Pleasure: Clubs and Societies

The variety of societies and clubs that sprang up in Victorian Bakewell involved all classes in the town, whether riding to hounds, singing in the choral society, playing on the wing for the Wanderers or entering a pig in the annual agricultural show.

Agriculture was still the principal form of employment in the surrounding area, though not in the town. There was, as we have seen, great interest in the North Derbyshire Agricultural Society, which occasionally held its show in Bakewell.

The Town Band in an Oddfellows parade along Matlock Street, c.1905. George Chadwick, the trombonist on the left, lost two sons (one of whom plays beside him) in the First World War.

However, some of the local farmers wanted a society more centred in the Peak and on Bakewell. In 1843 Lawrence and Peter Furniss of Birchill Farm posted the following notice in Bakewell and the surrounding farms:

It is the undoubted opinion of a number of practical farmers that it would materially promote the interests of agriculture to establish for the district of Bakewell a Farmers' Club. For this reason a meeting will be held at the Rutland Arms, Bakewell, at twelve o'clock, the 20th day of February instant, to organise and establish

an institution of the above description, to be called the Bakewell Farmers' Club.

The new club was set up and in 1850 broke away from the North Derbyshire Agricultural Society, organising its first show in the cattle market in October. So began the regular Bakewell Show.

White's Directory of 1857 extolled these early shows:

Bakewell Farmers' Club… may now rank amongst the most influential in the Kingdom, being liberally supported by the nobility and gentry of the district who contribute also largely to the prize fund. The object it has in view is the promotion of agricultural improvement for which purpose the members meet monthly for discussing every subject connected with practical agriculture and annual premiums are given to every description of farming stock, poultry, cheese, root crops, best cultivated farms, etc. There is also an excellent library attached to the Club, supplied with all the best works and periodicals in agriculture… The annual exhibition of stock is held at Bakewell… and all other meetings of the Club are held in the Rutland Arms Hotel. At the annual exhibition in 1856 the Silver Cup, presented by Sir Joseph Paxton MP for the best cultivated farm was awarded to Messrs Furniss, Birchill Farm.

In 1864 the Bakewell Show moved to the recreation-ground and in 1926 to its present site on Coombs

The Bakewell Field Club outside Eyam church, c.1895.

Bakewell bridge, January 1857. The town prepares to greet its new lord, Charles Cecil John Manners. Around the arch it reads 'GOD BLESS HIS GRACE THE DUKE OF RUTLAND'.

Road. The Club changed its name to the Bakewell Agricultural Society in 1874. It had admitted poultry in 1857, dogs for the first time in 1878 and merged with the Bakewell Horticultural and Industrial Society in 1898.

The interest in hunting also had its roots in local farming activities. The Duke of Rutland, of course, had a renowned pack of hounds at Belvoir, from which Mr Thornhill of nearby Stanton in the Peak acquired a small pack in 1848. After a few years the pack was sold to Robert Nesfield, the duke's agent in Bakewell. He built kennels well to the rear of his house at Castle Hill with a cottage for the kennel master and a boiling room. With an injection of other strains of hound the pack became known as the High Peak Harriers and hunted hares over the limestone uplands. William Greaves, portly landlord of the Rutland Arms and hunt secretary, began the tradition of taking the Boxing Day stirrup cup in the Square. The Hunt drew a wide membership from the gentry and farmers between Bakewell and Buxton and its social occasions were held in both towns.

At the opposite end of the social scale was the Order of Oddfellows, a fraternal society of working men whose origins in Britain extend to the mid-eighteenth century. A Bakewell branch, the Loyal Devonshire Lodge (no 396), was established in Water Lane in 1844 at a time of growth of friendly societies in the country. It first met in the New Inn Progress Works in Buxton Road and subsequently in the Market Hall. The Lodge, which owned property in the town and supported its subscribing members in times of sickness, poverty or old age, built houses at Oddfellows Terrace at the top of North Church Street which were let at low rents to the members. Their Lodge was in the building which is now the Gospel

The Duke and Duchess of Rutland welcomed at the bridge for a Primrose League meeting, 1891.

Bakewell Choral Society.

PRESIDENT—THE REV. E. T. BILLINGS, M.A.
VICE-PRESIDENT—S. TAYLOR-WHITEHEAD, ESQ., J.P., D.L.

A

CONCERT

Will be given in the

Town Hall, Bakewell,

ON

Thursday, December 20th, 1894.

Principal Performers:

MISS ADA LEE,
(OF MANCHESTER).

MRS. FULLER,   **MISS SEVERN WALKER,**

MISS E. TAYLOR.

MR. LACEY A. PARKER,
(OF DERBY).

MR. J. SMITH.

Violins—MISS MELLOR, MR. CALVERT.
Viola—MR. CLEPHAM.   Cello—MR. BROWN
Harmonium—MR. E. IRELAND,
Pianoforte—MISS K. TAYLOR.

Conductor - - Mr. T. B. MELLOR.

Doors open at 7-30 p.m., Concert at 8.

TICKETS—Reserved and Numbered, 2/6; Second Seats, 1/-; Third Seats, 6d., may be had at Mr. Wardley's, (where a plan of the Room may be seen) and of Members of the Society.

CARRIAGES MAY BE ORDERED FOR 10-15.

PROGRAMME.

✦ PART I. ✦

Selections from Mendelssohn's "Elijah," "St. Paul," "Hymn of Praise," "Athalie," &c.

MARCH ... ... "Cornelius" ...
THE BAND.

From "Athalie"   TRIO AND CHORUS, "Hearts feel that love Thee" ...
MISS ADA LEE, MRS. FULLER, AND MISS WALKER.

"S. Paul"
{ CHORUS ... ... "Happy and Blest." ...
{ AIR ... "But the Lord is mindful of His own." ...
     MRS. FULLER.
{ CHORUS ... "How lovely are the Messengers" ...

"Hymn of Praise."
DUETT & CHORUS ... "I waited for the Lord" ...
MISS ADA LEE AND MRS. FULLER.

"Elijah"
{ AIR ... ... "If with all your hearts" ...
     MR. LACEY A. PARKER.
{ QUARTETT ... ... "Cast thy Burden" ...
     MRS. FULLER, MISS WALKER,
     MR. L. A. PARKER, AND MR. J. SMITH.
{ TRIO ... ... "Lift thine eyes" ...
     MISS ADA LEE, MRS. FULLER, AND
     MISS E. TAYLOR.

"Elijah."
{ CHORUS ... ... "He watching over Israel" ...
{ AIR ... ... "O rest in the Lord" ...
     MISS WALKER.
{ CHORUS ... ... "He that shall endure" ...

SOLO & CHORUS ... "Hear my prayer" ... ...
MISS ADA LEE.

Interval.

✦ PART II. ✦

CHORUS with SOLO "Now Tramp o'er Moss and Fell"   *Bishop*
MISS ADA LEE.

SONG ... ... "O'er the hills of Normandie" ... ... *Faye*
MR. LACEY A. PARKER.

INTERMEZZO ... "Cavalleria Rusticana" ... *Mascagni*
THE BAND.
(By kind permission of E. Ascherberg and Co.)

SONG ... ... "The Jewel Song" ... ... *Gounod*
MISS ADA LEE.

SONG ... ... "Anchored" ... ... *Watson*
MR. J. SMITH.

PART SONG "Good night, thou glorious Sun" ... *Smart*

✦ God save the Queen. ✦

Bakewell Choral Society concert (1894) given soon after the opening of the new Town Hall.

Hall next to Oddfellows Terrace. Members held an annual feast and the funerals of deceased colleagues were usually followed by a supper. The Lodge ceremonies, rituals, initiation rites and titles were not unlike those of the freemasons. In the town they brought colour to many processions with their uniforms, rods of office and painted banners. They merged with the Derbyshire Peak Lodge in Chesterfield in 1990, though there are still subscribing members in the town today.

Different again were the cerebral and recreational activities of the Natural History Society, comprising the professional men of the town – teachers, doctors, clergy and lawyers. It was established about 1890 by Storrs Fox, the founder of St Anselm's Preparatory School. The members roamed the hills studying flora and fauna, geology and local history, and helped to maintain a small museum which Storrs Fox set up in his house.

Nor must we forget the political clubs, the male dominated manifestations of the Liberal and Conservative Parties. The former looked to Chatsworth and the Dukes of Devonshire as the representatives of the Whig and Gladstonian liberal tradition. The Liberals in the town were drawn to meetings in the duke's village at Edensor. However, Bakewell was largely a Tory town and its lord, the Duke of Rutland, still exercised a firm, if weakening, hold on his tenants. He allowed the party faithful to open the rooms upstairs in the Bath House as a Conservative Club. Here was a reading-room, smoking room and library, in short, a sort of gentlemen's club. Dominating the reading-room was the marble bust of Benjamin Disraeli, Earl of Beaconsfield, founder of the modern Conservative Party. The great icon, which was feather-dusted daily, represented the Bakewell branch of the Primrose League. This organisation, founded by Lord Randolph Churchill and John Gorst, was not officially part of the Conservative Party, though many leading Tories, such as the Duke of Rutland,

supported it. It celebrated Disraeli's birthday every year and sported the primrose, the flower he is said to have adored. The League promoted what it believed had been his political philosophy, to widen Britain's democracy. To this end women were welcomed into the League and were invaluable in organising teas, fêtes and excursions! However, they had to wait until 1918 to be given the vote at the age of 30 and another 11 years to be enfranchised at 21. By then the League had lost its appeal, though it still has an office in London.

Many of the clubs and societies availed themselves of the premises in the new Town Hall built in 1890. A choral society which had its origins in the Parish Church choir used the new assembly room regularly. Religious and secular concerts were conducted under the bâton of successive church organists, pantomimes were produced at Christmas, and dances and public meetings were held there.

Sport

The English passion for organised competitive games largely dates from the second half of the nineteenth century, although bat and ball games were eighteenth-century village pastimes and kicking a ball towards a goal stretches back much further. In the public schools of Victorian England boys organised their own ball games and invented rules for them. They took their new games up to the universities and then to the towns and villages where they worked as teachers, clergymen, doctors and businessmen. So leisure life in Bakewell was enhanced by new sporting clubs. The earliest was the Cricket Club, founded in 1861. Games were played across the river on the '20-acre' field, now the showground, to a body of rules which had evolved in village green play.

Gradually a mixture of professional men, businessmen and workmen formed the Bakewell Cricket Club which, soon after its foundation, came to play

Two pictures of the Bakewell cricket team, c.1890.

Bakewell ladies' cricket team with male captain and umpires, 1896.

Perhaps the earliest photograph of Bakewell's football team, c.1880. The blue and white quartered shirts are in the style of Blackburn Rovers. The rec's first pavilion, with adjoining lavatories, is little more than a shed.

Bakewell football team (c.1890) outside the house in Water Street of Robert Orme, wine merchant and grocer, who came to Bakewell from Coventry in 1844. The back row includes: *W. Charles, R. Blackwell, Revd Fuller, G. Birley, C. Marsden, T. Spencer, A. Taylor, S. Orme, M. Gregory, T. Mellow, G. Allsop;* middle row, left to right: *T. McGregor, G. Blagden, J. Hill, E. Thorpe;* front row: *H. Ford, W. Pollit, R. Barton.*

on the recreation-ground, where the Duke of Rutland allowed a rough wooden pavilion to be erected near the site of the present public lavatories. Unfortunately the club's records for this early period have not survived, though one or two photographs have. Playing in whites was not yet *de rigueur* and, as can be seen, the club members can hardly be considered sartorially elegant on or off the field! By the end of the nineteenth century the club included a 'Thursday side'. This was made up of shopkeepers and tradesmen who were unable to play on Saturdays but could turn out during half-day closing. A women's team also played under male supervision and, from a surviving photograph of the 1890s, was somewhat better attired than the men.

The Football Club was founded in 1878, interestingly in the same year as the Working Men's Club, which was set up in the vacated schoolroom in the old Town Hall. Just before the club was officially established, a match was arranged between a Bakewell side and one from the Working Men's Club on Shrove Tuesday. A sizeable crowd turned out in a field along Coombs Road to watch a good kick and rush contest.

The driving force in arranging this fixture derived from the public school and university men in the town. Stanley Orme, son of the founder of Bakewell's famous wine and groceries emporium, had played football at Ockbrook, a minor public school near Derby. He was instrumental in organising and playing in the side known as Bakewell Wanderers. Significantly, the name was taken from the famous public school side, the Wanderers, and the Bakewell team's colours were Oxford blue and black. The Working Men's Club was captained by the Revd F. Churchill, curate of the Parish Church. His team of 12, made up of artisans and workmen, beat the 12 men of the Wanderers 1–0.

Unfortunately, as with the Cricket Club, the early records of the Wanderers have been lost. However, on their 50th anniversary in 1928, *High Peak News* published information about their foundation and reported some early matches. We learn that games were played with as many as 16 a side and the goals consisted of two poles and a tape to act as a cross-bar. One regular bone of contention was the offside rule. Bakewell tended to play to this, following the

Founder members of Bakewell Golf Club, 1899. Standing, left to right: *P. Suggett, A.G. Taylor, C.H. Brooke-Taylor, D.S. Swanston, H. Severn;* seated: *V.R. Cockerton, C.W. Taylor.*

London Association rules. Other local sides preferred the rules of the Sheffield Association, which did not recognise offside play. Each side provided an umpire and, if these controlled the game with a different set of rules, the chaos that ensued is not difficult to imagine. Here, for instance, is the report in the *High Peak News* of the return game with Cromford, played at Bakewell on 15 March 1879:

Bakewell won the toss and chose to play against a strong wind in the first half. Then arose the question, 'What rules are to be played?' The Bakewell secretary had written on the 11th inst. to inform their Cromford friends they wished to play 'offside rules', meaning [those of] the London Association. The same evening the Cromford secretary wrote (the letters crossing) saying 'I want you to know that we play the same game that we played at Cromford in November last,' referring to the Sheffield Old Association not-offside rules. That occasion being the first time the Bakewell Club had ever played to the Sheffield rules and only yielded because they were on the Cromford ground, although it was against their interest and they lost 3–0...

The Cromford backs made some near shots at the goal

of the home team. The home forwards were continually following the leather in the opposite vicinity, showing some good play and the ball was at last placed between the posts for Bakewell. The home umpire (Herbert Littlewood) mistaking the visitors' goal keeper (who was standing with several others near the goal) gave his verdict, 'Offside!' But immediately perceiving his error, withdrew his decision and claimed the goal for Bakewell. Soon after this halftime was called and the visitors declined playing further except by their own rules and eventually left the field... It is recorded that the mistake was made by the umpire owing to the fact that the Cromford goalkeeper was in plain clothes.

Such were the early capers in the primitive days of football in Bakewell. The Football Association had been founded in 1867 but it took some years before its rules were universally accepted by the small clubs.

Some consider that golf was originally brought to Britain by the Romans and others that it originates in sixteenth-century Holland ('golf', 'put' and 'tee' are of Dutch etymology). Others again claim the Royal Blackheath Golf Club, purportedly founded in 1608, owed its origins to the new Scots king, James I. Whatever its derivation, golf was well established with accepted rules when it was first played in Bakewell in 1880. This late date is surprising in that it was a game for the well-to-do, who could afford a set of clubs as well as the green fees. The reason for its late arrival was not lack of interest, but the want of a good site for links. The sloping valley sides at Bakewell might provide some length for a few holes here or there, but certainly not the width for a circuit of 18 holes.

Would-be golfers took to the high ground on Calton pastures, where they contended with the rough grass and cattle droppings on the 'fairways' and some marginally better 'greens' on a nine-hole layout. After a few years of frustration, lost balls and broken clubs, these pioneers gave up for the time being. By the late 1880s a few of these early stalwarts tried again, led by Vernon P. Cockerton, a young solicitor practising in Bakewell and living at Riversley, in Castle Street. A native of Birkenhead, he had caught golf fever whilst watching the game played at nearby Hoylake. Cockerton and his friends cast their eye on the rough pastureland extending from the railway station to Coombs Farm in a narrow, sloping strip between the woodland and the railway line. The Duke of Rutland was sympathetic to Vernon Cockerton's overtures and, after his agent had secured the agreement of tenants, a strip of land 2,400 yards long was leased for the construction of a nine-hole course. There was not a clubhouse but an agreement was made with Robert Hage to use his wooden tearooms, soon to become Bakewell's first cinema, beside the railway station.

The first general meeting of the new club was held on 1 December 1899 in the council chamber of the new Town Hall. The founding members were principally from the prominent families of Cockerton, Taylor, Brooke-Taylor, and Cross. Vernon Cockerton became the secretary, G.H. Carmell the captain and the Marquess of Granby the president. Women were involved from the start, including the redoubtable Miss Constance Cross, and although a ladies' captain was not appointed until 1923, the golf club was up and walking. Hage's tearooms were vacated in 1905 and the present clubhouse began to be developed from the old kennels of the High Peak Harriers below Ball Cross. Though still a nine-hole course with little prospect of extension, it is one of the prettiest in England.

A Late Architectural Flourish

If such wealthy individuals as Archdeacon Balston and the Allcards could attract the services of great Victorians like Pugin and Paxton, Waterhouse, Scott and Butterfield, lesser local architects were responsible for the major rebuilding of the town at the end of Victoria's reign. If the Georgian era saw Bakewell improved with the odd good town house and some run-of-the-mill shops and houses, the somewhat romantic ideas of the late-nineteenth-century architects gave the town a rather hard-nosed Gothic flourish. Fanciful gables with ball finials in seventeenth-century manor-house style vied with battlements, oriel windows, a tower and even a mock portcullis.

Needham's saddlery, Bridge Street, 1890s, with Charles and Mary Needham from Flagg on the right. These premises were rebuilt at the turn of the century.

The Old Pudding Shop, later called The Original Pudding Shop, the Square. Bakewell puddings were made and sold here by the Wilson family in the last quarter of the nineteenth century, though they do not originate here.

Allen's Drapery, the Square, 1890s. Fred Allen stands in the doorway on the left.

The manorial style, shades of Bagshaw Hall, was used for the premises (now the HSBC Bank) of Andreas Edward Cokayne, an antiquary and writer on the Peak. He sold books and 'art pottery', besides maintaining a library and a museum of local archaeological finds. Across the road, also of the early 1890s and in a similar style, the new Crompton and Evans Union Bank sprang up at the junction of Water Lane and the Square. These two premises in ashlar made a stark contrast with the run-down, random limestone buildings around them.

Bakewell badly needed a new Town Hall. The old Market Hall, although extended and adapted for civic use, was quite inadequate. A new council chamber, public assembly room, magistrates' court and holding cells were essential. The Duke of Rutland was agreeable to demolishing derelict premises in Anchor Square and to contributing to the new building which, according to Andreas Cokayne, was much influenced by Haddon Hall.

There were other promoters who had a vested interest – the town's freemasons. Their Lodge, number 2129, had been founded in 1887, with the Duke of Rutland's backing, at a meeting in the Long Gallery of Haddon Hall and, somewhat surprisingly, it was named the Dorothy Vernon Lodge. Its members installed Andreas Cokayne as its first worshipful master and afterwards travelled by horse-drawn charabancs to a banquet at the Rutland Arms. The Lodge had no fixed meeting place and used various hostelries in the town. According to its records:

Burgons Stores, Bridge Street, c.1900. This and other shops were built on the front of Denman's house, which had later served as William Kay's private Grammar and Commercial Academy.

Bennet Needham with his wife Ellen at his wheelwright's shop at Milford, c.1899. The site is now part of a garage.

Joseph Smith's printing shop in the Square.

Building the Post Office, 1893/94. The central figure in the bowler hat is Thomas Allsop, builder, of Woodbine Cottage, Coombs Road. The lad to the left is Billy Wilson from the Old Pudding Shop. Sammy Welch holds the leading dray horse to the right.

The newly built Post Office and Town Hall, late 1890s.

Bath Street, 1880s. The upper floor of the new Town Hall rises over the run-down buildings.

Bath Street, 1880s. The Bath House is on the right. The barns were soon to be cleared to make way for Lady Manners Grammar School.

The third Lady Manners School in Bath Gardens. Note White Watson's tufa summer-house on the right.

Lady Manners Grammar School morning assembly in the Town Hall, 1899.

Lady Manners girls doing gym in Bath Gardens, c.1930.

Grand Concert for the opening of the new Town Hall, 1890.

The house and business premises of Andreas Edward Cokayne, antiquary, art collector, stationer and writer of such travel guides as Bakewell *and* A Day in the Peak. *The premises house the HSBC Bank, once the Midland Bank, at the time of writing.*

This building, too, though in an admirable situation, was sadly closed after 100 years to become yet another shop.

The Post Office was initially to have been built across the road beside the new Town Hall. However, this site, between Anchor Square, Bath Street and Bath Gardens, was considered a better location for a re-established Lady Manners School. More run-down cottages and outbuildings were duly swept away and the architect, Morewood Longsdon, drew up plans for a building to blend with the new Town Hall. Robert Nesfield laid the foundation-stone on behalf of the 9th Duke of Rutland and the duke and the duchess opened the new school on 22 September 1896.

The original terms of the Grace Lady Manners Foundation were changed. No longer was admittance restricted solely to boys from Bakewell and Rowsley. A total of 50 boys and girls were enrolled and the notion of co-education caused quite a stir in the locality. Foundation scholars from the area were admitted free, the other entrants paying a fee of £2 per annum, which quickly rose to £7 by the end of the century.

From the outset the facilities of the school were never adequate. Morning assemblies were held in the Town Hall's assembly room, games were mostly played on the showground and later on Shutts Lane, with tennis in Bath Gardens, whilst the annual sports day was held on the recreation-ground. As numbers on the school roll increased, some teaching had to be conducted in rented premises about the town. A boarding house was eventually set up in Archdeacon Balston's large vicarage. Nevertheless some children made considerable journeys to school by rail from as far north as Buxton and as far south as Belper. Among those travelling the latter route from Cromford was Alison Uttley (née Taylor), who won a scholarship in 1887. She went on to read science at Manchester University, but is best known to the world for her autobiography of her childhood at Castle Top Farm and her famous children's stories about Sam Pig and Little Grey Rabbit.

So Queen Victoria's reign drew to a close with an architectural flourish and great celebrations in the town both for her golden jubilee in 1887 and her diamond jubilee ten years later. On both occasions a tent was erected in the market-place, where a roast beef dinner was served to the men and boys over 14 years old, with a meat tea for the women and the girls over 14. Every schoolchild was presented with a commemorative mug. Proceedings began in the morning with a procession to church for a service of thanksgiving and ended with fireworks in the evening. In 1887 an oak tree was planted on the recreation-ground and in 1897 a fine cast-iron gas lamp was erected in the Square. The hospital and the swimming bath proposed by many had to wait.

Four years later, amid the gloom of the Boer War, the queen died. The loyal townsfolk mourned her passing and worried about the fate of their sons in South Africa.

Bakewell at the end of the nineteenth century from the golf course. The station is behind the walled clumps of trees on the right and Hage's tearooms, used as the golf clubhouse, are in the central foreground. Castle Hill and Station Road are undeveloped and Moor Hall is devoid of housing. Bakewell is still largely a riverside town.

The new fire engine, 1912. Though still horse-drawn, this was equipped with a steam-driven pump. It was paraded in the town's carnival following its replacement by a motorised vehicle.

Howard's cycle shop next to their smithy in Bridge Street, 1904.

who by 1896 was giving 'employment to a considerable number of hands'. When, in 1904, Groom sold the lease of the yard to Robert Smith of Castle Street, it was known as the Rutland Works and, though marble production had ceased, the timber yard was a success. Timber sawn here by a water-powered turbine was used to restore the nave roof of the Parish Church and replace the roof of the great hall at Haddon.

More important in terms of jobs was the new development of the cotton mill site. Its owner, the Duke of Devonshire, sold it in 1898 to the DP Battery Works of Charlton, which had been making stationary batteries for railway stations and country houses since 1888. The new factory took on labour as

demand for such batteries increased and it became the town's chief employer, eventually having a workforce of 300.

In those seemingly Indian summer years of the Edwardian era one thinks, as did A.E. Housman, of the happy childhood and youth of many whose lives were soon to be cut short. Bakewell still possessed something of the rural idyll soon to be lost forever. We read of youngsters paddling and swimming in oxbows of the river, and tickling trout in the bankside shallows. The brown trout and grayling were now augmented by a strange North American species, the rainbow trout, inadvertently released into the river in about 1900. This was the only place in the country where it had managed to breed naturally.

Holme Bank chert mine, 1920.

Holme Bank chert mine's carnival float, c.1920. Sammy Welch is holding the horse.

Outdoor pursuits had been uppermost in the mind of Robert Baden-Powell, a British officer and Army scout who had served in the Boer War. As a member of the beleaguered British garrison at Mafeking his military scouting and ability to improvise enabled the besieged to hold out successfully against considerably superior forces for 217 days. He returned to England a hero and began the scouting movement in 1907.

Inspired by his example, Sidney Allcock, head of Bakewell Boys' Church of England School, introduced the principles and practice of scouting to his pupils and two patrols were formed. The new vicar, Revd R. Griffiths, encouraged his parishioners to enrol their sons, as did the other clergy of the town. On 9 June 1910, the Bishop of Derby chaired a meeting in Bakewell Town Hall with the aim of establishing a district association. He was elected its

Jim Wigley carting a block of chert out of Holme Bank, 1920. The industry was dangerous; gunpowder was employed to extract large blocks from the thick chert beds.

Timber dray leaving Bakewell Station for Smith's woodyard, c.1922. This oak log was specially ordered for the restoration of the north nave aisle roof of the Parish Church.

president, Colonel Brooke-Taylor its chairman and the vicar its secretary; Sidney Allcock and Storrs Fox, who introduced scouting to St Anselm's School, were among the committee. Within a year six Scout troops were formed, involving some 50 boys.

The Girl Guide movement, founded in 1910, received similar support in Bakewell. In 1919 a company of Guides and a Brownie pack were formed and these still thrive at the time of writing.

The cinema was also a novelty, for adults as much as children, and in 1912 a colourful impresario came to town looking for likely premises. This was one Louis de Burgh, who had managed the Hippodrome at Southend as well as a music hall in Berlin. He lit upon Robert Hage's tearooms by the railway station, which had recently been relinquished by Bakewell Golf Club. He leased the rooms and on 27 August 1912 he opened the grand-sounding Picture Pavilion. Performances of silent films were given nightly at 9p.m. with additional showings on Saturdays at

3p.m. and 7p.m. We do not know what pictures were first shown in these rudimentary surroundings, but Charles Bradbury has left us an amusing account of off-screen activities:

I think his name was Devine [he means de Burgh] who first showed pictures in the tin-roofed shed near the station. In spite of the discomfort the place always seemed full. It was gas lit, and when Devine got hard up he ran a length of rubber tubing to the lamp standard near the station yard to get a free supply – until he was caught. It was amusing to hear people reading the script [i.e. the sub-text of the silent films] to those who couldn't read at all.

The greatest fun was the orchestra which consisted of old Mr Fewkes, piano, Mrs Thompson, the postmaster's wife, violin, and her daughter, cello. The orchestra used to be on the right of the screen behind a green curtain. You could just see the tops of the players' heads. Mr Fewkes was bald and had a lump about as big as half an

Bridge to Smith's woodyard and the old marble works, c.1910.

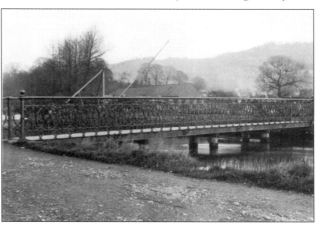

'The Iron Bridge' to Smith's woodyard.

Aerial view over Bakewell, 1924. Beside the DP Battery Works in the foreground is the gasworks. Beyond the town the River Wye still oxbows through its unbuilt-up meadows. At the top of the photograph a plume of smoke indicates a train approaching the station.

Minden and Braeside cottages with grass thatch, c.1900. They were rebuilt soon after this photograph was taken.

egg on his head which was a target for orange peel.

Mrs Thompson was also a singer and, to the surprise of everyone, she often crashed out to a scene which took her fancy. Mr Fewkes (who often played and sang in the pubs) would join in singing bass. I shall never forget them singing the Volga Boatmen, when most of the audience joined in.

Dick Allcock, son of the headmaster of the Boys' School, gives us a picture of the happy life of a young boy growing up in this period and the way he even-

tually responded to the patriotic call in 1914:

Life was confined to town activities, mainly provided by the religious bodies, with regular periodic diversions provided by the bustle of cattle and produce markets, the fairs, Volunteer Reviews and the visits of travelling concert and theatre companies and circuses. Provided for the evening hours of the (12–18 years) youth were football, cricket, sports, a gymnasium, a Church Lads' Brigade, Boy Scouts and camping... Hooliganism, vandalism and juvenile delinquency were practically unknown. The practice of poaching was confined to about four well-known characters of middle age.

Many boys, on reaching the age of 17, began to think about joining one of the TA organisations, either the 6th Sherwood Foresters or the Derbyshire Yeomanry. Most of my friends joined the former, but I, yearning to ride a horse, plumped for the latter and for a hectic series of weekends, with other pals, learned to ride, how to cope with a .303 rifle (I was already a good shot with a .22) and how to stand on my own feet among young and older men from other parts of Derbyshire.

My father was... a keen but fair disciplinarian, who took a leading part in many of the out-of-school youth activities. And perhaps my brother, sister and I led somewhat sheltered lives but with reasonable freedom... My allowance at 16 years of age was 2s. [10p] a month. A visit to the picture house would cost 3d. [1½p].

For me, on the whole [I had] a very full and happy

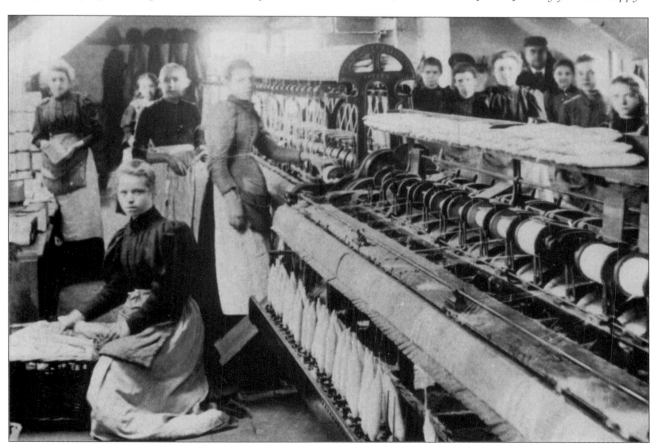

Cotton spinning at Melso works, c.1920.

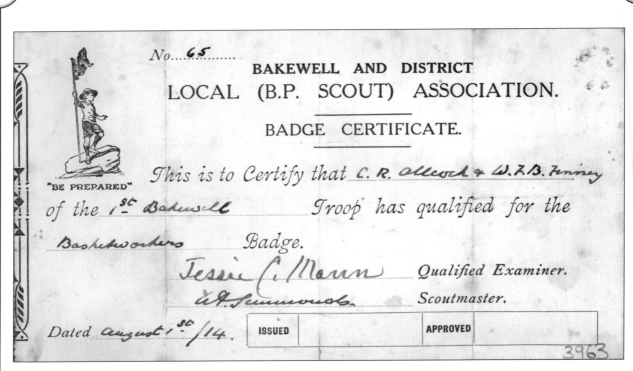

Dick Allcock's scout badge certificate for basketwork, 1 August 1914.

The Boys' School orchestra, c.1920, in Bath Gardens.

The cinema near the station, 1921–31.

The Anchor Inn decorated for the coronation of George V, 1911.

May Day celebrations at Holme Hall, 1924.

Fly-fishing on the Wye, c.1920.

Escaped circus elephant shot by the military, 1905.

Methodist Sunday school celebration of May Day, c.1910, at Thomas Allsop's Woodbine Cottage on Coombs Road. The boy on the left, shouldering a sword, is Arthur Bramwell, whose father ran the coal business in the station yard.

Bakewell from Castle Hill, 1920s.

childhood, passing through the local elementary schools on to the local grammar school, followed by employment in September 1913, as an unqualified teacher at the local Boys' School. In February 1913 I joined the B Squadron of the Derbyshire Yeomanry... In 1914, after a colourful February Yeomanry Ball at Derby, we prepared for the annual camp due to be held on Salisbury Plain in the September...

The First World War

Dick Allcock did not go to Salisbury Plain. In August 1914 he and his fellow troopers were called up in readiness for embarkation.

War was declared on 14 August 1914 and the territorial battalions and yeomanry regiments had been mobilised two days earlier. Bakewell had been like a busy anthill. The horse fairs ceased as animals as well as wagons and carts were requisitioned to provide second strong mounts for the yeomanry and haulage for the supplies and artillery. The Rutland Arms yard was the assembly point. Supplies were loaded, men lined up in full kit in the Square and all made ready to depart by road or rail.

'D' Company 6th Battalion Sherwood Foresters had marched out of Bakewell for Chesterfield on 9 August. After further training the battalion, including the company from Bakewell, eventually sailed from Southampton to Le Havre on 26 February 1915 as part of the 46th North Midland Division. The Derbyshire Imperial Yeomanry formed part of the 2nd Mounted Division and were shipped to Egypt for action against the Turks.

Bakewell, in the summer of 1914, was now a quiet, anxious town. The fairs ceased. The Bakewell Show, organised for 5 August that year, was barely a token gathering. The government had cancelled all excursion trains and farmers themselves were barely able to move about. Their workers were volunteering to fight, horse boxes and cattle wagons had been requisitioned and there was an urgent need to get the hay and corn harvests in before men went away. Some exhibitors drove their stock on foot for distances of ten or 12 miles to reach the show. Thereafter no more shows were held until 1920.

Tradesmen feared for their businesses as the war dragged on and more men were needed. John Littlewood, Boer War veteran and now a sergeant, joined his old regiment, the Sherwood Foresters. Dick Allcock tells us that his own father, the headmaster of the Boys' School, had enlisted many volunteers for that regiment. Then, in October 1914, he marched off to Buxton with his newly formed company to help form the 2nd/6th Battalion of the Sherwood Foresters. Dick's brother, still at Lady Manners School, joined him in the Yeomanry.

Nor were women idle. Dick's mother and his

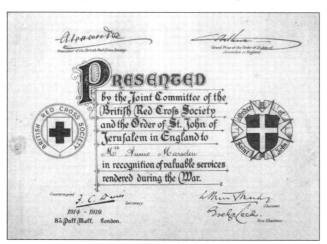

Certificate of commendation to Mrs Annie Marsden, of Birchover and Bakewell, for Red Cross service in the First World War.

A service in Bakewell Square following the outbreak of the First World War, 1914.

sister, like other women in the town, worked for the Red Cross in local hospitals. Women in Bakewell also helped in early munitions work at the DP Battery factory after 1916. In that year the Admiralty, having commissioned more submarines, required more batteries. Chloride Batteries had hitherto held the monopoly but the Bakewell company was now given a share in the production. Meanwhile, in their differing spheres of operations, the soldiers from the parish and those around were serving with bravery and distinction.

After training in Egypt, the Derbyshire Yeomanry were required for the disastrous Dardanelles campaign. Leaving their horses behind, they were shipped to Suvla Bay on the Gallipoli Peninsula on 17 April 1915. Almost immediately they joined the ill-fated attack on Chocolate Hill and sustained heavy casualties. These increased in the ensuing trench warfare, either from Turkish gunfire or from disease. When the campaign was abandoned the Yeomanry were transported back to Egypt to be reunited with their horses.

They were then, in the spring of 1916, shipped to Greece to fight in the Salonika Campaign. Here they were in intermittent combat with the Bulgarian Army, chiefly in the Struma Valley. Trooper Joe Mansfield of Bakewell won his Military Medal in a cavalry action which saw the loss of 15 in his troop of 20. Sergeant Briggs had three horses shot under him

before he himself was killed. However, the Bulgarians surrendered to the Yeomanry in September 1918, their white flag now being kept among war memorabilia in Bakewell's Old House Museum.

The Sherwood Foresters fought on various parts of the Western Front, from Ypres to the Somme, and the regiment suffered appalling losses. 'C' Company from Bakewell saw their first action in 1915 on the Ypres salient and were in and out of the trenches in that area for the rest of the year. In one incident Privates Marsden, father and son, were both wounded by the same bullet. Casualties rose. Private Hubert Fewkes from Buxton Road was killed. Lance Corporal Large of Diamond Court was wounded at Kemmel, as were Private Benjamin Wilson at St Eloi and Lieutenant Donald Storrs Fox, son of the headmaster of St Anselm's School, at Comines Canal, whilst having breakfast.

Both the battalion and 'C' Company, under the command of Captain Wheatcroft, distinguished themselves in the three-day battle for the Hohenzollern Redoubt. Two Military Crosses were won in this action, one of them being awarded to Second Lieutenant William Lyte of Bakewell, who had just been promoted from the ranks for distinguished service.

On 1 July 1916 the battalion was engaged in the Battle of the Somme, where it lost 170 of all ranks on

Sergeant John Littlewood of the Sherwood Foresters receives his long-service medal.

John Littlewood and Joe Loveday, whitesmiths, at the door of the forge in Granby Road, c.1910.

the first day and in 1917 it was barely out of the line, during which time Privates James Cooper, Bert Birley and Robert Chadwick, all of Bakewell, were killed. Finally, at Béthune in 1918, 'C' Company was involved in the attempt to break through the Hindenburg Line at Bellenglise, where further gallantry by Private Johnson and Lance Corporal Tanner saw the award of two further Military Medals.

And then, on the eleventh hour of 11 November, hostilities ceased. The servicemen came home to church services of thanksgiving and street celebrations. Lieutenant Donald Storrs Fox arrived in Bakewell in the middle of the night. Finding his parents' house locked and in darkness he forced his way into the school's dormitory and frightened the boys! Next day there was general rejoicing.

Some servicemen never enjoyed such delight. Of the 517 who left Bakewell parish 70 never returned. The burning question now was how to honour and remember these lost heroes. A roll of honour was kept and their names were read out on Armistice Sunday, but their only civic memorials were bunches and wreaths of flowers placed in the Square by relatives, friends and comrades. This was remedied in 1920 when the local branch of the Royal British Legion was founded. It was decided to remove the lamp set up for Queen Victoria's diamond jubilee and replace it with a stone war memorial in the form

115

Armistice Service in the Square, 1918.

Armistice Day, 1919. Those in mourning placed wreaths on the railings of Bath Gardens. The First World War cenotaph was erected in the Square and that commemorating those killed in the Second World War and the Korean War is within Bath Gardens.

Bakewell clergy, 1920s. Standing, left to right: Revd G.H. Wilson (Primitive Methodist), Revd F.T. Leaton (Congregationalist), Revd Bansall (C of E), Revd J.W. Vaughan (Wesleyan Reform), Father Firth (Roman Catholic); seated: Mrs Brayshaw (Friends), Revd E. Spink (vicar), Revd T.H. Sheriff (Wesleyan Methodist).

Bakewell Cottage Hospital.

The opening of Bakewell Cottage Hospital by the Duke of Rutland.

of a cross. On the base were recorded the names of the fallen.

The cenotaph became the focal point in the centre of the town. As motor traffic increased the Square could no longer accommodate the town fair. Gradually the cenotaph became what it is today, the centre of a busy traffic roundabout. However, all traffic ceases on Armistice Sunday to permit the two minutes' silence and the laying of poppy wreaths.

The larger memorial to those who fell in the Great War was the Bakewell War Memorial Cottage Hospital, which was built by public subscription. The town had long needed a hospital and various doctors and town medical officers had pressed the matter. In 1920 the Duke of Rutland, who had given a plot of land off Butts Road, laid a foundation-stone along with one laid on behalf of the Dorothy Vernon Lodge of Freemasons. The names of the 263 men from the district who made the supreme sacrifice are recorded at the entrance. Now, 85 years later, it no longer serves as a hospital but is a private nursing home for the elderly. Nevertheless, the names of the fallen remain, undisturbed and unforgotten.

Twenty Years of Peace

Those who had the good fortune to return after the First World War quickly settled into their old jobs and the town began to bustle again. It was the age of the motor car and some who had served in mechanical

The cenotaph which replaced the 1897 jubilee lamp in 1920.

Congregationalist children's pantomime, c.1936. Back row, left to right: *Clifford Cowen, Victor Broomhead, Harty Hudson, Doreen Hirst, Dorothy Ashley, Mrs Welsh, Eddie Welsh, Victor Fox;* third row: *Bill Buer, Janet Bramwell, Audrey Cowan, Margaret Woolley, Annie Broomhead, Edna Blackwell, Jean Fox, Jean McGregor, Ivy Noton, Margaret Cowan, Lilly Buer;* second row: *Olive Blackwell, Dorothy Weeldon, Jean Naylor, Jean Weeldon, Delia Peters, Margaret Blackwell, Brenda Hanley, Mary Welsh;* front row: *Ralph Weeldon, Geoff Hanley, Ronald Davies, ? Hanley, Roy Fox, David Hanley.*

units were equipped with skills which were to serve them and the community well.

One such was Murdoch Mackay. Obviously not a local man, this enterprising Scot, born in Edinburgh in 1883, began work as a forester and eventually came to work on the Chatsworth estate about 1910. Whilst attending a dance in Bakewell's Town Hall, he met Jane Anne Shenton, from Stanedge Road, daughter of a local shopkeeper. Early in 1914 they left the Parish Church in a carriage and pair and settled down briefly to married life in Matlock Street. When war broke out Murdoch travelled north again to Inverness and enlisted in the Cameron Highlanders.

Returning to Bakewell at the end of the war, he became a lorry driver and subsequently drove the town's fire engine and its ambulance. In 1919 he purchased his first vehicle, a Maudsley, and began a local coach and taxi service. This was the origin of Bakewell's first motorbus service. Gradually he built up a small fleet of vehicles, including a 20-seat open tourer, all of which were garaged in Granby Croft. It was his proud claim that he operated from Bakewell the country's first 'mystery tours' at half a crown (12½p) a head. He certainly operated the town's first bus service to Sheffield, eventually selling it to Sheffield City Corporation for about £1,000. In the 1930s he even purchased a 1926 Rolls Royce, which

was used not only for weddings and funerals but also for outings as far afield as Blackpool.

Tradesmen and businesses were increasingly turning to motorised vehicles. This was especially true of Orme's, in the Square. Their trade in groceries, and especially in wines and spirits, expanded substantially, as did the radius of their delivery service. Their premises were too cramped and lacked the modern amenities befitting what had become the most prestigious food store in the Peak. In 1936 the Urban District Council permitted Orme's to demolish the seventeenth-century Hall in the Square, the most imposing building in the town after the Parish Church. Some Georgian shops were also taken down to allow Orme's new premises to extend round the corner into Matlock Street.

So the Square took on the appearance it has today. The fairs were no longer held there, nor some of the old public meetings. The rising volume of traffic prevented such gatherings. However, the High Peak Hunt took its Boxing Day stirrup cup outside the Rutland Arms until the outbreak of war in 1939. The harriers were brought down from their new kennels in Shutts Lane.

The other event which was to close the Square to traffic once a year was the annual carnival, held in July. The origins of the carnival, like those of the Bakewell Town Band which accompanied it, are

Bakewell Square, c.1910, showing hackney carriages with tourists at the foot of North Church Street.

uncertain. Both are said to date from before the First World War. Whatever their true age they have both been a constant source of pleasure and amusement. Traditionally the carnival has been graced by a carnival queen who, with her attendants, is driven at the head of a procession of horse-drawn or motorised vehicles, each decked with colourful and comic floats contributed by the shops, businesses and organisations in the town. From the collections for charitable causes from the crowds lining the streets donations were made towards the fund to provide the town with its long-awaited swimming pool. At the time of writing the carnival is the largest of its kind in the county.

The most significant change in the inter-war years was undoubtedly the Duke of Rutland's decision to sell almost all his property in the town and some of his land to the east of it. This, of course, meant the

Murdoch Mackay standing beside his taxis, 1920s. The car on the left was for the Sheffield service, while the one on the right, named Dorothy Vernon, was for more local use.

The Rutland Arms coachyard and its new garage, c.1920.

end of the lordship of the manor of Bakewell. There were various reasons for this decision. First, the town was now self governing with an elected council and the old feudal manorial court was virtually defunct. Secondly, and more importantly, was the economic decline of the landed estates in England brought about by the increased taxation, including heavy death duties, imposed by Lloyd George's Liberal government. In addition, the end of the First World War saw a rise in labour costs and a depreciation in land values. A third of Derbyshire's great estates were broken up by 1930.

So the duke sold off his peripheral Bakewell estate at an auction in the town in 1920. Under the hammer went the Rutland Arms, his agent's house at Castle Hill, the old marble works and timber yard, the corn

Carnival preparations on the rec, c.1930. T.H. Howard's new garage is in the background and beyond is open land.

Orme's vans, 1929. Deliveries were made as far as Staffordshire and South Yorkshire. The head office was in Bakewell and branches were established at Darley Dale, Matlock, Chesterfield, Sheffield, Derby, Stoke and Stafford.

The building of Orme's new store, Matlock Street corner, 1936.

The corner of Matlock Street and the Square, c.1936, now demolished.

mill and numerous houses and plots in the town. The golf course, as we have seen, and Wicksop Wood beyond, were also sold. He did, however, retain his fishing rights in the River Wye.

Next, the duke looked to Haddon Hall and the surrounding estate at Rowsley, Alport and Youlgreave. To maintain this as an entity he, and especially his wife Violet, had encouraged his eldest son, John, to live at Haddon and run the estate. As a schoolboy of 12 years of age, John Manners had romanticised about moving back to Haddon after a family absence of two centuries.

In 1921, following the great sale in Bakewell, the duke deeded Haddon Hall to his son, now come of age and Marquess of Granby, thus hoping to avoid the possible financial blow of death duties. The new marquess set to work painstakingly to restore the house. A new roof was placed on the great hall,

The Square from Matlock Street corner, late 1930s.

The Clothing Hall, 1935.

the panelling throughout the house was reset and repaired, the windows were skilfully re-leaded and newly acquired antiques were used to augment what remained of the splendid medieval, Elizabethan and seventeenth-century furnishings. Local craftsmen from Bakewell were employed to make one of the earliest and most sympathetic conversions for reoccupation.

At first visitors were encouraged and ticket prices were raised to assist with the costs of reconstruction.

However, the marquess found it difficult to cope with the numbers, the parking problems and the litter. He looked for quiet and privacy. First he reduced opening times and then, to keep 'trespassers' away, he closed the local footpaths which crossed his land and three in particular which circumvented his house and gardens.

Local rambling clubs were incensed and Bakewell Urban District Council, supported by the Rural District Council, took physical action. Having, out of

The Square and Orme's new store, 1947.

Bakewell Town Band on the recreation-ground, 1920s.

The carnival queen and her attendants enter the Square, 1934. Note the town's fire engine passing the Red Lion. The Clothing Hall, on the right, is empty in readiness for demolition.

Orme's carnival float enters the Square, 1938. It was designed by Joe Hawkins, the window dresser, who is in front directing the driver.

Carnival queen, 1940s.

The Guy fire engine, 1920s, with (in the centre) *the chairman of the UDC and the clerk, V. Cockerton; Jim Rogers* (seated second from right, front row); *Eddie Smith* (seated top left) *and his brother Cecil* (front row, third from left).

Arthur Cresswell's butcher's shop in the Market Hall, Christmas 1922.

Sale at H. Broughton's shop ('established 1784') in King Street, 1930s. This high-class business became known as 'The Fashion House of the Peak'.

The Marquess of Granby's coming of age, 1907. Seated between his parents, the Duke and Duchess of Rutland, the marquess had been deeded Haddon Hall, pictured here, which he began tastefully to restore.

The Duke of Devonshire (centre) *opening the new cricket pavilion on the recreation-ground (1929). Stanley Orme, who presented the pavilion to the club, is seated on the right.*

Portrait of the Marquess of Granby, 1907.

courtesy, informed Alexander Carrington, the marquess's agent in Bakewell, that he intended to break down any notices and barriers closing the footpaths, Vernon Cockerton, the town clerk, mustered his forces at Bakewell bridge. Accompanied by William Davies, surveyor to the UDC, he assembled eight workmen armed with crowbars, shovels, pickaxes and wire cutters, and set off along the river bank followed by some 200 townsfolk and ramblers. They cut through barbed wire, made gaps in fences and stone walls and broke the locks off gates. The small army marched some eight miles unopposed and were back in Bakewell in three hours.

The marquess responded swiftly by suing the two councils. They in turn sought legal representation and the case was heard in the Chancery Division of the High Court. The case for neither party was clear cut and, though counsel for the marquess clearly demonstrated that the three footpaths around Haddon Hall had been legally stopped up in 1799 and again in 1813, he could find no legal grounds to enforce the closure of the others. It was decided to settle out of court. The marquess had won, at the most, a pyrrhic victory. The two councils felt vindicated in keeping open most of the footpaths and the marquess agreed to pay their costs.

He had, however, been allowed to plant screens of trees which, whilst changing the appearance of the landscape, cocooned his new residence from the traffic on the A6 and the ramblers in the adjoining meadows. In 1925 he succeeded as the 9th Duke of Rutland and finally moved in, promptly closing the house to the public except for one day each year in support of local charities.

Fortunately, little lasting animosity was engendered by this legal wrangle. The duke still performed some historic duties in the town and

Bakewell Bowls Club celebrates its tenth anniversary, 1930. The photograph was taken in Bath Gardens in front of White Watson's tufa summer-house (now demolished).

The Melso ladies' cricket team (on the right), captained by Daisy Fisher, prepare to play the Progress Works (on the left), captained by Ena Darnell, 1920s.

The Melso works' outing, 1930s.

Bakewell's Orpheus Operatic Choir, 1940s.

exhibited his generosity in various ways. A bowling club had been set up in 1920 to play on what had been the tennis courts in Bath Gardens of Lady Manners School. Further recreation was encouraged when, in 1923, the duke and the Marquess of Granby gifted to Bakewell UDC the recreation-ground, known originally as Horsecroft Meadows. Here, since 1884, various games had been played, the Bakewell Farmers' Club had assembled its annual show and the annual carnival parade had been organised.

Now cricket and soccer thrived and the recreation-ground catered for both. In 1929 Stanley Orme gave a new pavilion to the Cricket Club on land already donated by the Duke of Rutland, and this allowed the old one to be removed and replaced by a park shelter and public toilets. Cricket not only flourished in the town but was especially strong in the schools in the inter-war period. St Anselm's School, despite its small number of boys, built up a strong tradition. Coaching by the staff was excellent, as were the wickets prepared by the enthusiastic George Beard, head groundsman until his retirement in 1975, and by his successor, John Hudson. Some of the boys went on to play for their public schools, universities and the English counties.

Cricket and sport in general at Lady Manners School improved appreciably following the acquisition of new playing-fields, well removed from the school on Shutts Lane. Thanks to the unfailing support of Reg Harvey, who was a master for more than 50 years, an Old Mannerians Association was set up in 1931. Until the outbreak of war it put out teams to play cricket, rugby, hockey and tennis. Rugby became the winter sport of the boys at Lady Manners School and the Old Mannerians carried the flag for rugby in Bakewell, and still do on their ground off Coombs Road. One of their members, Gil Hudson, who also shone at cricket and rugby, went on to represent Derbyshire, the Midlands, England and Great Britain at hockey.

In 1936 Lady Manners Grammar School was removed from its inadequate premises in the centre of the town and re-housed in new buildings in Shutts Lane. No sooner had the school settled in than war was declared on Germany on 3 September 1939.

The Second World War

Men went away to join the Armed Forces and as they did so others came to Bakewell to join a new regiment. On 11 September a troop train pulled into Bakewell Station and from it alighted three companies of fairly raw recruits. They formed up and marched down to their requisitioned quarters at Burton Closes and Haddon House. One company had been raised at Chesterfield and two at Glossop. Among the latter was Leslie Wright, now Colonel Wright, who still lives in the town at the time of writing.

The three companies were designated 4th Corps Signals, that is the Signal Regiment to the 4th Army Corps, to be commanded by General Sir Claude Auchinleck. Their commanding officer at Burton Closes was Colonel 'Gerry' Underwood, an old Harrovian who had served in the First World War. He kept morale high despite the initial lack of water, bedding and greatcoats. So spartan were the conditions in the overcrowded billets that the Corps suffered a serious influenza epidemic as well as an outbreak of spinal meningitis. The Cooperative Hall in King Street and the Union Workhouse building served as hospitals, where local volunteer nurses tended the invalids.

Having completed their training, the 4th Corps Signals left Bakewell to form part of Auchinleck's North Western Expeditionary Force, which tried, unsuccessfully, to oust the Germans from Norway in 1940. In their place came 6th Corps Signals, commanded by Colonel Harry Spencer. The officers' mess was now established at Brooklands on Coombs Road and Nissen huts were erected behind Burton Closes to ease the accommodation problem.

After the British Army's amazing evacuation from the beaches around Dunkirk between 27 May and 4 June 1940, Britain braced itself for a German invasion. In Bakewell some 700 soldiers were in training and these were increased by the local Home Guard, which was recruited after May 1940. The police, too, were on invasion alert and their numbers were increased by the recruitment of special constables, one of whom was First World War soldier Dick Allcock. At night air-raid wardens patrolled the streets to enforce blackouts, these last officers being put to the test in 1940 when, on 12 and 15 December, Chesterfield and Sheffield were heavily bombed. No one anticipated an air raid on little Bakewell, quietly tucked away in the Wye valley. However, German intelligence was aware the DP Battery Works was hard at work completing Admiralty contracts. At 6p.m. on 23 December a German aircraft circled over the town and dropped two high explosive bombs.

Richard Cockerton, the town clerk, was dining at Burre House. He dashed from his home, across Bakewell bridge and alerted the ARP (Air Raid Precaution) centre in the Town Hall. Those on duty had already summoned the town's fire brigade to the DP Battery Works. The bombs had narrowly missed the factory's mill dam, leaving two large craters and minor blast damage to houses in the Lakeside area.

At 8.35p.m. a series of explosions was heard in the area between Conksbury and Youlgreave as a load of incendiary bombs rained down on the countryside. A farm was hit but otherwise there were no casualties. The blackout had been effective, though the Luftwaffe no doubt considered the surprise raid had been a success.

The Glossop Company of the Royal Corps of Signals, based at Burton Closes.

Colonel G.J. ('Gerry') Underwood, commanding officer of the Glossop Company, Royal Corps of Signals.

Mother Goose *pantomine in the Town Hall, 1940s.*

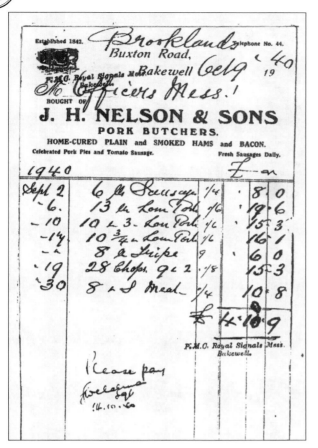

Butcher's bill for the officers' mess at Brooklands, 1940. Although the government had introduced rationing, it does not yet appear to apply to the officer class.

Colonel Leslie Wright.

Bakewell and District Home Guard, 1940s.

The town suffered no further air raids and continued to play its part in the war effort. Its British Legion and Red Cross kept in touch with local servicemen abroad, sending letters and such food parcels as rationing at home would allow.

Various premises in the town were requisitioned by the government to accommodate the troops. As well as at the camp at Burton Closes they were billeted around the town in Bath Street, Bridge Street, Buxton Road and Haddon House. The Castle Hotel, Red Lion, Peacock, Queen's Arms, Manners Hotel, Royal Oak, King's Arms in Buxton Road and the Devonshire Café in Church Alley all took in soldiers. The officers' mess was established briefly in the Rutland Arms and then at Stanton Woodhouse, near Rowsley, before moving to Burton Closes and Brooklands in Coombs Road. The Ministry of Food commandeered slaughterhouses in Bath Street and set up Food Control offices in Catcliffe House.

The strain on the town's medical facilities was alleviated by establishing the Medical Inspection Centre in Bottomley's House (now Red House), in The Avenue. Evelyn, Duchess of Devonshire, organised a Voluntary Aid Detachment Hospital in the Co-operative Hall in King Street.

Gradually, as the tide of war turned in Britain's favour, the Corps of Signals evacuated Burton Closes. The Royal Army Service Corps then replaced them before they too moved into action. The premises were not empty for long. Following the D-Day landings in Normandy in 1944, thousands of German prisoners of war were shipped to England and makeshift camps were hastily prepared. The Nissen huts at Burton Closes were made ready to receive prisoners from various transit camps. The Bakewell camp was placed under the command of Lieutenant-Colonel Victor Holland of the Royal Signals. The POWs were given various tasks to perform, from helping in Bakewell's parks and gardens to farm work, clearing snow in winter and assisting foresters on the Chatsworth estate.

Among those in the camp was Wolfgang Rudolf, a submariner in the German Navy who was taken prisoner in Boulogne by the Canadians after the D-Day landings. He was a charming young man from Dresden who spoke a number of languages and had a good command of English. His account of life in the camp is interesting and amusing. The régime was mild, the food grim and the Nissen huts freezing in winter. The prisoners were given a dog which was passed around at nights as a source of warmth. Wolfgang used his charm with the camp's commander and was allowed the use of a gun to keep down rabbits in Chatsworth Park, many of which were brought back to feed his compatriots and their dog, whilst some were traded in the pubs of Bakewell. Wolfgang frequented the Manners, where he quickly made friends with the locals and occasionally brought back a packet of Woodbines to keep Lieutenant-Colonel Holland agreeable.

In 1945 victory parties were held in the town and the returning soldiers were fêted. Wolfgang himself had no such joyous prospects should he return to Dresden. The beautiful city, almost razed to the ground by the RAF, was occupied by the Russians. He stayed in Bakewell, married a local woman, did various useful jobs in the district and died in 2002, a British citizen who appeared more British than his adopted compatriots – Bakewell's symbol of Anglo-German reconciliation.

Meanwhile, the names of those who fell in the Second World War are recorded beside the heroes of the First on a cenotaph in Bath Gardens. At the time of writing Armistice Day is still recognised by the laying of poppy wreaths, and Colonel Leslie Wright, who came to the town as a young recruit in 1939, still dons his bowler hat and shoulders his umbrella to conduct the parade.

Prisoner-of-war camp, Burton Closes.
(WATERCOLOUR BY POW WOLFGANG RUDOLF, C.1945/6)

Wolfgang Rudolf, German submariner, with his cousin, Werner, on leave in Dresden, c.1940.

CHAPTER 7

Fifty Years of Change

Bakewell changed dramatically in the 50 years after the war and became quite a different market town, socially, politically and economically. If the influence and control of the Manners family reached its nadir after the First World War, that of the gentry and professional classes met the same fate after the Second.

The numerous fine town houses could no longer be maintained. With the exception of Burre House, still the residence of the Cockerton family, and Holme Hall which, despite frequent changes of ownership, surprisingly continues as a private residence, the rest were adapted to a variety of other uses.

Burton Closes, like most houses that had been subjected to military occupation, had become a run-down estate and was put up for sale in lots. The house eventually became a nursing home, the stables became flats and the park and gardens were developed for private housing. Private nursing homes were also established in Balston's large Victorian vicarage and at the Barkers' late-Georgian residence, Brooklands, on Coombs Road. Indeed, nursing homes were the most common solution for large empty premises as the ageing population of the town and district increased. Thus the town's cherished Cottage Memorial Hospital became a private nursing

home, as did neighbouring Gernon Manor. Newholme Hospital continued to serve National Health patients.

The doctors in the town also gave up the large houses which had doubled as surgeries and consulting rooms. Thus Dr Emerson held his last surgeries in Church House before joining the new team medical practice in its purpose-built medical centre in the Butts. In King Street, Catcliffe House became a job centre and the house of John Taylor, Bakewell's first banker, became a Cooperative Store and then an antiques centre. In 1951, on the foundation of the Peak District National Park, Britain's first national park, Aldern House became its headquarters. A new element of what was to be a reorganisation of local government in the area was now in place and would have a part to play in Bakewell's future planning and development.

The imposing houses once occupied by the Duke of Rutland's agents were no longer private residences. Bagshaw Hall became the town's Conservative Club and then was restored to house an architectural practice. Its stables were converted to housing, as was its walled garden. Castle Hill House was vacated by the Blake family after the war and operated briefly and unsuccessfully as a country club before being purchased in 1953 by Derbyshire

Buses in the Square, c.1947. A North Western bus is departing. In the right foreground are one of Hulley's buses from Baslow and a Silver Service bus from Darley Dale. Hulley's company is the only one still operating.

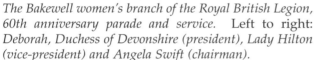

The Bakewell women's branch of the Royal British Legion, 60th anniversary parade and service. Left to right: *Deborah, Duchess of Devonshire (president), Lady Hilton (vice-president) and Angela Swift (chairman).*

Reg Nelson, Bakewell's last pork butcher, and his famous pork pies.

County Council and opened as a boarding house for Lady Manners School. Sold to a private developer 50 years later, at the time of writing it is being converted into flats.

Old families such as the Bosleys, Barkers, Taylors and Allcards, who had helped govern the town for three centuries, were gone. Bakewell's Urban and Rural District Councils carried on after the war in the face of a growing belief in governmental circles that local government in the counties was in need of reform. The Local Government Act of 1974 abolished Urban and Rural District Councils and allocated them to District Councils – a new tier of local government beneath County Councils. Bakewell now became a Town or Parish Council of nine elected councillors who in turn elected a mayor from their number and appointed a paid part-time clerk.

The new District Council, initially known as West Derbyshire, and later as Derbyshire Dales, extended from Ashbourne to Taddington and included the towns of Wirksworth, Matlock, Tideswell and Bakewell. The electors of Bakewell found their old self-governing powers removed to the new District Council at Matlock. The town was allocated three seats on a council which in 2005 numbers 39, but was delighted that Roy Bubb (1934–88), born and educated in the town and Clerk and Chief Finance Officer of the old Urban District Council, became the Chief Executive of the new Derbyshire Dales District Council. He died prematurely and is commemorated by a sundial in Bath Gardens.

The District Council took over Bakewell's principal assets, which had been acquired from the Dukes of Rutland – the cattle and stall markets. It also assumed control of the recreation-ground, the cemetery, the Bath House and Bath Gardens. The workforce associated with these areas, together with refuse collection and street cleaning, also passed into the hands of the District Council. Bakewell's town council was left with such areas of the town as Scot's Garden, beyond the town bridge, the ancient monument site of Castle Hill, Parsonage Field, left to the town as a recreational area, Ball Cross Woods and small pockets of land at Endcliffe and below the cemetery. None of these was an asset in terms of income and the Town Council depended for its principal source of finance on an annual precept from the rates now set by the District Council in Matlock.

The Victorian Town Hall, once the focal point for concerts, plays and dances, was a financial burden as its community use declined. It suffered a great blow in the year 2000 when, following the Lord Chancellor's legal reforms, its Magistrates' Court was removed to Chesterfield.

Frank Lomas, the coal merchant operating from the station yard, 1950s.

Otherwise the town continued to expand. Private housing developments extended the town in two directions, to the north-east and the south-east. The former consumed the old estate of Castle Hill House from the railway station and the house itself to Newholme and beyond; the latter spread over the parkland of Burton Closes beneath Burton Edge and along the Haddon Road. In addition to this, community housing was laid out at Highfields, beside the Moorhall estate, in the 1990s.

Trade in Bakewell changed rapidly after the war, as did the business community. The old craft-based businesses and shops such as blacksmiths, whitesmiths, saddlers and shoemakers, wheelwrights and carriage makers, already disappearing before the

war, no longer adorned the pages of the town directories. The sweet shops, haberdashers, ironmongers and paint shops vanished and the number of specialist butchers declined from six to two. The shopkeepers who formerly lived over their premises, or in the locality, had largely sold out to non-residents from Sheffield, Chesterfield and Derby and their staff came in by car from miles around. The town's chamber of trade died out in the 1990s.

The town's old yards and passages were improved and developed into shopping arcades. So Water Lane and Water Street, once largely residential areas, were taken over by lock-up shops with store-rooms above. New developments such as Portman Square, Granby Arcade, Hebden Court and King's

Quail & Mellor's gentlemen's outfitters in the Square. Registered as Quail & Bucknell in 1890 and Quail & Mellor in 1895, the shop finally closed in 1994.

Court became enclaves for boutiques and cafés largely catering for the burgeoning tourist trade. The era of the small delicatessen and the wine shop had arrived to provide foreign food and drink which more and more people had come to enjoy while holidaying in sunnier climes. Established shops such as Broughtons in King Street and Quail & Mellor in the Square finally succumbed to the new competition after over a century of trading, whilst the last of Bakewell's great grocery emporia, Orme's, finally left the premises it had rebuilt in 1936, on the corner of the Square and Matlock Street, to make way for Bakewell's first supermarket.

Pubs closed, too. The Royal Oak in Matlock Street was pulled down to make way ultimately for more shops there and in Granby Road. The taproom of the

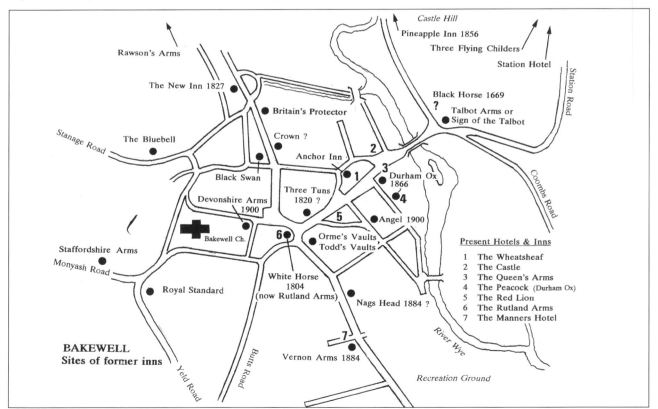

Sites of former inns and those now remaining.

Denis Sutton, for 50 years a vet in the town, judges the pets' competition at the carnival. He is assisted by Maisie, his wife.

Rutland Arms, once part of the stables of the old White Horse, was briefly the town's second fish and chip shop before quickly becoming a shop specialising in patchwork fabrics. The Rutland Arms itself, that great tavern of the coaching era, lost its social pre-eminence and was no longer the gathering place of the farming and fishing fraternities, though it remains the town's only hotel. The Wheatsheaf in Bridge Street was pulled down and indifferently rebuilt. Together with the Peacock, the Queen's Arms, the Red Lion, the Castle and the Manners, it still remains open all day on Mondays to cater for the dwindling number of farmers and a growing throng of tourists.

Bakewell Town Council, 1974. Standing, left to right: John Riley, Reg Evans (mayor), Harold Higgins, Victor Littlewood; seated: Maureen Carey (clerk), Ernest Brown, Eddie Welch, Fred Peacock.

Relaying track between Bakewell Station and Coombs viaduct, 1962. The line was soon to close and later became the Monsal Trail.

Taking up the track at Bakewell Station.

Demolition of Bakewell's last cinema, 1973.

Yet Bakewell kept its four banks, not so much now for the farming community as for the growing population of the town and the villages around. The purpose-built Post Office, excellently located with the banks in the Square, lost its prominent position after 100 years and vanished from view into a new store in Granby Road. Its former premises became another shop.

Against the general tide of change one man tried to look backwards in time in order to establish a unique kind of town house and business. In 1953 Maurice Goldstone, an antique dealer and specialist in English oak furniture, purchased from the Thompson family their old chemist's shop with outbuildings to the rear. The main premises were probably Elizabethan in date and fronted King Street with a charming double bow-windowed façade of 1780. By adapting run-down eighteenth- and

Kenning's garage, May 1965. The Granby Road car park now occupies this site.

Bath Street and New Street (off to the left) before their demolition in the early 1960s.

Post Office and telephone staff, 1947, with (seated in the centre) Mr Fogg, the Bakewell postmaster. To his left are Winn Rowe, national telephone rep., George Rowland, postal telegraph officer and Miss E. Pardoe, exchange supervisor.

Plan of Bakewell Post Office, 1920s.

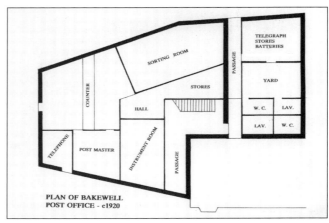

Avenel Court, King Street – a box-framed building erected after 1953 by Maurice Goldstone using old interior timbers from the Moon Inn at Stoney Middleton.

Accident in King Street, 1970. A juggernaut narrowly avoids Maurice Goldstone's antique shops in the old Town Hall and Avenel Court. Broughton's shop is not so lucky. Maurice Goldstone and his son Michael stand between the vehicles.

nineteenth-century outhouses behind his antique shop Goldstone cleverly created a pastiche of pseudo-medieval buildings and added a box-framed fifteenth-century extension, constructed from the internal timbers of the Moon Inn at nearby Stoney Middleton. To the interiors of these buildings he added stained glass, panelling and fragments of old oak staircases purchased at the many sales he attended. He furnished them with old oak furniture and draped the walls with tapestries and hangings. Although now converted into houses, shops and a café, named collectively King's Court, sufficient has been saved to allow visitors to dream, as he did, of a bygone age.

Unemployment

If the destruction by fire of Arkwright's mill was a huge blow to the town in 1868, the closure 100 years later of its successor, the DP Battery Works, was even more calamitous. The factory had produced large stationary batteries for country houses, Post Offices and for the Admiralty in the two world wars. It also helped to pioneer electrically powered vehicles. So successful had been the company that it was taken over by Chloride in 1928. However, after the war the factory struggled to remain competitive and in 1955 the larger of its two water-wheels collapsed in its 128th year. The cost of reconstruction proved prohibitive and both wheels, fragments of which are now exhibited in the Old House Museum, were

dismantled. In their place was installed a more economical electric turbine. All seemed well, but in truth the factory, now run by Exide and Kathenode Batteries, was still not sufficiently abreast of modern technology. With 300 employees at Bakewell, 1,500 in Manchester and 1,000 in Dagenham, the Bakewell plant was expendable. The four local MPs, for West Derbyshire, High Peak, Chesterfield and South East Derbyshire, met a deputation of the Transport and General Workers' Union at the House of Commons in a move to save the factory. This led to an appeal to Mrs Barbara Castle, Secretary of State for Employment and Productivity. All was in vain and by June 1970 the factory finally closed.

This closure coincided with those of the Holme Hall and Holme Bank chert mines in the late 1960s. They were the last and most productive of some 18 chert mines and quarries that had operated in and around Bakewell since the nineteenth century. The last two mines had employed 35 men after the First World War and 27 after the Second World War, with many generations of the same families working there. In 1995 an unsuccessful attempt by Gordon Bowring was made to establish a museum at Holme Bank as a memorial both to them and to a lost industry, but planning permission was refused.

Smith's woodyard, on the Rutland Works site, was the next to close and the cutting of high-quality timber by water-powered saws ceased, as had the production of marble on the site at the beginning of the century. Water-power had been used at the

Holme Bank chert quarry just before closure, c.1960.

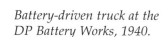

Battery-driven truck at the DP Battery Works, 1940.

The Working Men's Club in Butts Road before the buildings were converted in 1964.

The rebuilt premises of the Working Men's Club in Butts Road. The club, founded in 1878, previously occupied the upper floor of the old Town Hall, seen in the background.

Bakewell and Eyam Community Transport leaflet.

cotton mill, the DP Battery plant, the corn mill, the marble mill and the saw mill, long after it had ceased to be efficient and economic. All had closed.

Unemployment continued to rise following the closure in the late 1960s of the railway between Matlock and Buxton. Businessmen who could work in Manchester or Derby sold their houses in Bakewell and moved away. Freight was moved onto the local roads and rail passengers switched to cars as the decline in bus services left surrounding villages more isolated. Ironically there is now a move to reopen the line! Thankfully the gap in rural transport had, to some degree, been filled by the continuing services provided by Hulleys of Baslow and by the Bakewell and Eyam Community Transport scheme, established in 1988 under the capable chairmanship of Ian Green.

Education, Clubs and Societies

Like much else in the town, the state schools were moved like pieces on a chessboard until their re-organisation in the 1970s. The boys' secondary school moved into the premises previously occupied by the girls' secondary school at the rear of the Church of England Infants' School in Bath Street. The girls were transferred to a new site of prefabricated classrooms opposite Lady Manners School at the junction of Shutts Lane and Monyash Road. The Methodist Junior School, the principal feeder school to Bakewell's three secondary schools, was moved to new purpose-built premises on Burton Edge, near Lady Manners School.

Then, in 1972, Lady Manners School ceased to be a selective grammar school. The new comprehensive school absorbed the staff and pupils of both the boys' and girls' secondary schools, together with pupils of sixth-form age from Hope Valley College. The new school had expanded from 650 pupils to twice that number by 1980 and in 2005 has 1,468 pupils on the school roll. Despite expansion on the Shutts Lane campus, the school's accommodation was and still is inadequate for its numbers.

As for the town's independent school, St Anselm's, its pupil numbers also increased. This was partially due to the introduction of comprehensive education by the surrounding local authorities, quite apart from the school's academic and sporting reputation. The school also strengthened its position by opening a pre-prep department in 1976 and became co-educational in the same year. A nursery department opened in 1992 and at the time of writing there are 278 pupils on the roll aged from two and a half to 13. To cope with this expansion a new games-field and then a sports-hall and additional classrooms were created.

Meanwhile, adult education classes, which had been organised since before the war by the Workers' Education Association, were now reinforced by courses run by the Department of Continuing Education at Sheffield University. Sadly, government policy was responsible for the closure of these non-award-based university courses in 1994. To fill this vacuum nationally an independent organisation called the University of the Third Age (U3A) was established. Following a meeting held in the Town Hall in 1998, a Bakewell branch was formed to organise self-teaching groups of retired people in subjects ranging from Latin to horticulture and from music to rambling. Its founding chairman was Meg Laird.

These adult activities have helped to support many of the town's more recent cultural societies. Pride of place must go to the Peacock Players. Originally known as the Old Mannerian Dramatic Society, it took its title from the crest of the Manners family and also of Lady Manners School – a peacock

The Peacock Players' Tudor carnival float, 1930s.

Bakewell Chess Club, 21 January 1947. Left to right, back row: J.T. Priestly, Len Mosley, H. Broughton, (president) J.W. Raine, secretary and head of the junior school, F.P.S. Garlick; middle row includes: M. Robson, D. Storrs Fox, Miss Baldwin, G. Baker, Dr A.H. Holmes; front row: A. Smith, W. Thomson, S. Milner, E.H. Milner, J. Parsons.

Bakewell Cricket Colts, Matlock and District League Champions, 1948. Left to right, back row: *Arthur Bramwell (umpire), Gerald Hudswell, Geoff Hudson (captain), Peter Hudswell, Michael Osbourne, Roy Bubb;* front row: *Lennox Brown, John Lupton, Jack Naylor, Bob Webster, David Hearnshaw;* sitting on the ground: *Billy Hudson.*

Bakewell Cricket Club 1st XI, c.1967. Left to right, back row: *Bert Hannaford, Jack Naylor, Ken Clark, Mick Beresford, Richard Corkhill, Ken Dunham, Roy Howes, Tom Hannaford (chairman);* front row: *Neil Mather, Graham Trivett, Roy Ballington, Gordon Roberts (captain), Gerald Worsencroft, Dennis Powell.*

Bakewell Football Club in their Arsenal strip, 1955. Left to right, back row: A. Keenan, G. Cooper, B. Thorpe, W. Sudbury, D. Bateman, R. Wardle, T. Tomlinson, A. Bramwell, W. Hudson, G. Stewart, F. Oliver, L. Twist, M. Morton; front row: M. Dawson, P. Moran, O. Bonsall, S. Wardle, W. Hulley.

Shire horses and drays in the parade ring at Bakewell Show.

The monthly magazine of the Association of Bakewell Christians.

The vicar of Bakewell, the Revd Edmund Urquhart, blesses the town's well dressings, 1986. This well, by the Brownies, celebrates the National Parks.

in its pride. In 1936 it premiered in Bakewell Town Hall a four-act play entitled *The Mysteries of the Corinthian Vase*, written by William Gosling, classics master at the school. The Players enlivened the sombre years of the war by performing the works of the great dramatists as well as pantomimes and homespun offerings. Great success was enjoyed by the Players after the war and in the 1970s Sue Stone, one of the members and an Old Mannerian, organised the Bakewell Youth Theatre, from which talented young people have entered the world of theatre, film and television.

One of the most successful societies established in the town since the war has been the Bakewell and District Historical Society. It was founded in 1954 by John Marchant Brooks, its first chairman, with the intention of saving from demolition Bakewell's oldest surviving house, the early-Tudor Parsonage House. Including among its founding members Maurice Goldstone, George Butler, artist and first treasurer, and the local builder, Charles Bradbury, it took the Parsonage House as its 'headquarters', restoring it over the last 50 years to become the Old House Museum. Run by the Society's volunteers, this, after the Parish Church, is now the principal visitor attraction in the town. The small band of members who gathered in 1954 had increased to 287 in the Society's golden anniversary year half a century later. Its research and publications over the

last 50 years have now culminated in this commemorative book.

Another fascinating museum has also opened – the M and C Motorcycle Collection, assembled and maintained by Peter Mather and Phil Crosby. It not only consists of vintage motorcycles but also exhibits much of the paraphernalia of the roads and garages in the early years of motorised travel.

The Association of Bakewell Christians (the ABC) was formed as a consequence of a small handful of Bakewell people, each from a different denomination, working together in 1965 to erect the first Christmas crib in Bath Gardens. It seemed a good idea to foster this ecumenical spirit, so the inaugural meeting of what became the ABC was held in January 1966. It is recorded that people joined 'as a group of Christians desiring to foster growth towards unity where possible and to take united action over Christian principles where possible.' This co-operation has continued to the present day and many will be familiar with its monthly publication, *Good News*.

One could expand further, if space allowed, on the other clubs, societies and organisations which have sprung up in recent years, such as the Photographic Circle, the Choral Society, the Bridge Club and the Civic Society. Suffice it to say that Bakewell has much of cultural interest for its residents and visitors and in 2005 launched an annual Arts Festival, to take place in August, which is enthusiastically supported.

The Bakewell Project

The 50 years after the Second World War witnessed considerable change in Britain's market towns and

Bakewell Cubs' training day, April 1969. Lunch break with Simon Hudson (left), Chris Wyatt and Paul Beedham.

Bakewell Brownies 2nd Pack making Christmas cakes for the elderly in Hoyle Court, 1998. Left to right, back row: Hayley Anthony, Philip Swift, Danielle Fisher, Angela Swift (Brown Owl), Claire Crofts; middle row: Jennifer Morewood (Snowy Owl), Jade Robinson, Jemma and Hayley Grant, Emma Smith, Kimberley Hannan, Rachel Pearson; front row: Alex Hardy, Lauren Thomas, India Cox, Emma Reeves, Holly Kennah, Poppy and Shona Russel.

The Old House Museum, Bakewell, celebrating the Bakewell pudding, 2000.

Bakewell was no exception. As standards of hygiene and animal welfare improved it was clear that the stall and cattle markets could not continue to occupy the same site. Especially so since the bustling days of the stall market in the 25 years after the war saw a greater variety of goods on offer and stallholders from a wide area beyond Bakewell. The four Bank Holiday Monday markets were highlights in the market's year, stalls spilling along the riverside and traders attracted from as far afield as London's Petticoat Lane, with consequent pressure on staff space and parking areas for traders' vehicles.

The West Derbyshire District Council was allowing the ancient charter market to spread beyond its traditional bounds and planning permission was sought for an extension across the river. At this point, in 1975, the stallholders organised themselves to form the Bakewell Market Traders' Association under the chairmanship of Trevor Smith. Thereafter, the schemes for expansion were discontinued, a new and fairer licensing system for pitches was introduced by the council and the new association was consulted on general market matters, especially on the fixing of stall rents.

The town was also now being clogged by traffic on market days, with cattle trucks finding it more difficult to enter the town and pass along Granby Road to the cattle pens and the lorry wash. A scheme to regenerate Bakewell and at the same time ease some of the town's traffic problems, put forward by the District Council in the 1990s, was known as the Bakewell Project. Central to the Project's aims was an attempt to halt the decline in sales of cattle by transferring the cattle market to a new site across the river, equipped with the most modern facilities. With farmers increasingly adopting other means of selling their animals and many cattle markets closing nationally, the plan was designed to ensure that Bakewell's would not suffer a similar fate.

Part of the original plan envisaging a bridge over the river from the end of Granby Road, of which no one in Bakewell approved, was shelved in favour of a bridge at the southern approaches to Bakewell. To raise capital in addition to European and other funding the council proposed to sell the old market sites to a property developer for the erection of

Bakewell stall and cattle market, 1980s. The building on the left with the hipped roof was the well-designed public lavatory.

Trevor Smith (right) and John Whibberley (centre), president and chairman of Bakewell Market Traders' Association, make a farewell presentation to Walter Musson of the District Council on his retirement, April 1998.

The Medway Centre. (ARCHITECT'S DRAWING, 1999)

housing along the river and to the Somerfield chain for a medium-sized supermarket. There was considerable controversy over the proposals. Local businessman David Coe organised and financed the 'Save Bakewell Campaign', which fought against the Project, whilst others, though aware of shortcomings in some of the details, considered it a well thought-out attempt to solve a difficult problem.

In spite of the opposition, however, the Project was completed and the Agricultural Centre was opened by the Princess Royal in 1999. It is for Bakewell's residents and visitors, together with future historians, to judge whether the town has gained or lost in consequence.

After almost a century of patient waiting and collecting money, Bakewell also gained a new swimming pool and above it accommodation for a library, which for many years had been housed in wooden huts. Particularly satisfying was the new Medway Centre, built on the old site and completed and fitted out inside by an amazing community effort directed

The new supermarket, built as part of the Bakewell Project. Initially Somerfield, it was subsequently sold and at the time of writing belongs to the Co-op.

The front of the Agricultural Business Centre, the present cattle market.

The sheep pens for the new market with their controversial roof, seen from Station Road.

by Alan Pigott as 'clerk of works'. Vic Pratley, chairman of the centre, had striven hard to get the whole enterprise under way. These joint efforts epitomised the old spirit of co-operation in the town.

Matlock Street and the entrance to Granby Road were smartened up with new shops, with flats over them, where the Royal Oak had once stood. On the opposite corner a small supermarket and other shops were erected on the site of the house and outbuild-

ings of Dennis Sutton, for many years a respected vet in Bakewell. Together with the successful monthly farmers' markets held in the Agricultural Centre, these have all helped to diversify the shopping in the town.

In the 60 years since the Second World War Bakewell has participated in the changes affecting Britain as a whole. There has been a decline in agriculture and in the town's importance as the

King Street in the 1970s, as recreated by the BBC for the filming of their production 'In Denial of Murder', 2003.

administrative centre and market town for the area, with some industries disappearing entirely and others growing to take their place. This is especially true of tourism; the trickle of visitors of former times, not all that distant, has now become a flood, Bakewell's geographical position making it easily accessible from the large centres of population which surround it. Some visitors come to take advantage of the excellent walking country within easy reach of Bakewell, whilst others come in order to shop. It is a very pleasant destination for all, surrounded as it is by superb scenery and with Chatsworth House and Haddon Hall as added attractions. For a long time, too, Bakewell was a residential town and this it remains, both for retired people, many of whom originally came here as visitors, and for those whose work takes them each day to the numerous neighbouring towns and cities. Change may be faster now, but the town has always been subject to it, as has been amply demonstrated in this book, and Bakewell will continue to confront its associated challenges, as it always has.

A characteristic view of Bakewell.

Subscribers

George S. Agutter (In Memory of), Bakewell, Derbyshire

Peter A. Bennett, Baslow, Derbyshire

Joshua Bennett-Keer, Baslow, Derbyshire

Andrew Beresford, Bakewell

Angela and Chris Birkle, London

Harry Blagden, Bakewell, Derbyshire

Janet Blagden, Bakewell, Derbyshire

John Bloomer, Bakewell, Derbyshire

Dr Paul R. Bowden

Gordon Bowering, Great Longstone

Wendy Bowering, Great Longstone

Stephen and Jane Bradbury, Bakewell, Derbyshire

Diane Bradwell, Bakewell, Derbyshire

Clare Brighton, London WC1

Mark Brighton, Kew Bookshop, Kew

John Brocklehurst, Bakewell, Derbyshire

A. Barbara Brooke-Taylor

G.W. Brooke-Taylor, Leamington Spa

Frank Brotherton, Bakewell

Nigel P. Brown, Bakewell

Paul A. Brown, Bakewell

James, Janet, Robert, Eleanor and Daniel Button, Rowsley, Derbyshire

Miss M. Cadge, Bakewell, Derbyshire

Margaret E. Cadge, Bakewell, Derbyshire

Mrs M. Cantrill, Baslow

Dorothy Margaret Capel (née Lomas), Thornborough, Buckinghamshire

Rachel Carrington, Bakewell

Major General P.B. Cavendish

George Challenger, Bakewell, Derbyshire

Barbara Chapman

Miss C. Clarke, Sheffield

Chris and Cath Clennell, Lowfell, Gateshead

Mr and Mrs J.G. Clifford, Eyam, Derbyshire

Stephen and Mandy Coates, Wenslees, Derbyshire

Michael R. Cockerton

Christine Cook, Eastwood, Nottinghamshire

Dr Justin Cooke, Ashford-in-the-Water

John Corbridge, Bakewell, Derbyshire

Antony Cox

Pamela Crump, Bakewell

Robert R. Cumming, Great Longstone, Derbyshire

Dr D. Dalrymple-Smith, Baslow

Miss M. Daybell, Buxton, Derbyshire

Roger J. Elliott, Bakewell, Derbyshire

The Revd Dr Lida Ellsworth, Bakewell

Patrick E. Erskine-Murray, Bakewell, Derbyshire

Eyam Museum, Eyam, Derbyshire

Susan Fletcher, Bakewell

The Franklin Family, Bakewell

Trevor Gibbons, Ilkley, West Yorkshire

Sue Goddard, Bakewell

Mavis Goldstraw, Bakewell

J.G. Goudie

David Grant, Bakewell, Derbyshire

Ian W. Green, Bakewell

George and Jan Hambleton, Baslow, Derbyshire

Fredrick J. Hamilton, Bakewell, Derbyshire

Kathleen R. Handley

David S. Hardman

Mr and Mrs G.W. Hewson, Beauchief, Sheffield

Monica Hickie, Baslow, Derbyshire

Susan and Michael Hillam, Bakewell

Monica A.A. Hills

Timothy A. H. Hills, Nottingham

Christopher W.W. Hills, Ilkley, Yorkshire

John F. Hollingworth, Ashford-in-the-Water, Derbyshire

Mr Andrew Hooton

Miss Angela Hooton

Mrs Patricia Mary Hooton (née Smith), Bakewell, Derbyshire

Ruth Hopkins, Bakewell, Derbyshire

Ronald Hopkinson, Monyash, Derbyshire

Catherine Dorothy A. Howard, Bakewell, Derbyshire

Mrs D.A. Howes, Metheringham, Lincolnshire

Paul, Jan and Alice Hudson, Morwenstow, Cornwall

Billy Hudson, Bakewell, Derbyshire

Susan E. Hudson

Frank Hurst, Great Longstone, Derbyshire

Emma and James Jenkins, Penwortham, Lancashire

Catharine Helen Jenkinson (née Lomas), Chesterfield
George William Keech, Bakewell, Derbyshire
Stephen C. Kehr, Bakewell, Derbyshire
Dr Mike Knapton, Cambridge
Laurence Knighton, Bakewell
Susan Lawes, Overstrand
Nick Longland, Bakewell, Derbyshire
Vicky Longland, Bakewell, Derbyshire
Jo Longland-James, Bakewell, Derbyshire
John R. Lupton, Walkington, East Yorkshire
Mrs Sylvia Marsden, Ashford-in-the-Water, Derbyshire
Sue and Jeff Marsh, Bakewell
Jo Martin, Bakewell, Derbyshire
Louis and Christine McMeeken, Elton
Pamela Jean Molyneux
Annette Moody, Bakewell, Derbyshire
Miss Jessie Nadin, Bakewell
David and Diane Naylor, Edensor
Jack and Freda Naylor, Bakewell, Derbyshire
John Naylor, Bakewell, Derbyshire
Philip Naylor, Christchurch, New Zealand
Carol Newsom, Bakewell, Derbyshire
Jan E. Newton, Bakewell, Derbyshire
T. Nuttall
Simon Ogg, Bakewell, Derbyshire
Mrs A.P. Orme, Bakewell
Mrs Bernice Owen, Kendal
Janita R. Palethorpe, Bakewell, Derbyshire
Arthur E. Palfreyman, Matlock, Derbyshire
Mrs Pauline Pearson
Deborah and Jonathan Pickering, Los Gatos, USA
Alan Pigott
Michael Pigott
Michael and Shirley Plant, Bakewell, Derbyshire
Mrs Oonagh K.M. Pocock, Over Haddon, Bakewell
Revd and Mrs Brian Pritchard, Bakewell
Dr and Mrs I.L. Pykett, Ashford-in-the-Water, Derbyshire
Les Rawson and Jackie Taylor, Bakewell, Derbyshire
C.J. Renshaw, Middleton Hall, Middleton By Youlgreave, Bakewell
Sheila M. Rhodes, Bakewell

Jill Roberts, Bakewell, Derbyshire
Jose Roberts
John N. Robinson, Bakewell
Robert E. Roe, Baslow, Bakewell, Derbyshire
Frank Saunders, Bakewell, Derbyshire
John and Hazel Saynor, Bakewell
John and Gillian Serocold, Putney, London
Paul A. Sheldon, Bakewell, Derbyshire
Catherine Sherratt, Little Bakewell, Derbyshire
Mrs Jacqueline Sigley
Arabella Smallman, Newmarket, Suffolk
Grattan Smallman, Walderslade, Kent
Jeremy Smallman, Finchingfield, Essex
John Smallman, Bakewell 1961–93
Jonathan Smallman, London
Sally Smallman, Bakewell 1961–94
Gerry W. Smith
Mr and Mrs Stuart Smith, Curbar, Derbyshire
Jan Stetka, Burton Closes, Bakewell
Mrs Betty Stevenson
Peter R. Street, Bakewell, Derbyshire
Professor John N. Tarn, Stanton-in-the-Peak, Derbyshire
Andrew Taylor, Bakewell
Elveen Taylor, Bakewell
Joseph Thacker, Bakewell, Derbyshire
D. and L. Thrower, Bakewell, Derbyshire
Philippa Tilbrook, Bakewell, Derbyshire
Richard and Ann Tomlinson, Bakewell
Rosalie Treece
Dr M. Anne Turner (née Broughton), Bakewell
Robert Tym, Ashbourne
Edmund and Diana Urquhart, The Vicarage, Bakewell
John F.W. Walling, Newton Abbot, Devon
Mrs Gwen Watt, Bakewell
Peter J. Watts, Bakewell
Harry and Barbara Weaving, Bakewell
Tony and Madeleine Westley, Bakewell, Derbyshire
Mr Jonathan Wicksteed, Bakewell, Derbyshire
Elizabeth Wilbur, Bakewell, Derbyshire
Margaret Willett, Chesterfield, Derbyshire
G. Norman Wilson, Youlgrave
The Wise Family, Bakewell, Derbyshire
Herbert Woolley, Bakewell
Rosalind J. Wright, Bakewell

Community Histories

The Book of Addiscombe • Canning and Clyde Road
Residents Association and Friends
The Book of Addiscombe, Vol. II • Canning and Clyde Road
Residents Association and Friends
The Book of Ashburton • Stuart Hands and Pete Webb
The Book of Axminster with Kilmington • Les Berry
and Gerald Gosling
Bakewell • Trevor Brighton
The Book of Bampton • Caroline Seward
The Book of Barnstaple • Avril Stone
The Book of Barnstaple, Vol. II • Avril Stone
The Book of The Bedwyns • Bedwyn History Society
The Book of Bergh Apton • Geoffrey I. Kelly
The Book of Bickington • Stuart Hands
The Book of Bideford • Peter Christie and Alison Grant
Blandford Forum: A Millennium Portrait • Blandford Forum
Town Council
The Book of Boscastle • Rod and Anne Knight
The Book of Bourton-on-the-Hill, Batsford and Sezincote •
Allen Firth
The Book of Bramford • Bramford Local History Group
The Book of Breage & Germoe • Stephen Polglase
The Book of Bridestowe • D. Richard Cann
The Book of Bridport • Rodney Legg
The Book of Brixham • Frank Pearce
The Book of Buckfastleigh • Sandra Coleman
The Book of Buckland Monachorum & Yelverton •
Pauline Hamilton-Leggett
The Book of Budleigh Salterton • D. Richard Cann
The Book of Carharrack • Carharrack Old
Cornwall Society
The Book of Carshalton • Stella Wilks and Gordon
Rookledge
The Parish Book of Cerne Abbas • Vivian and
Patricia Vale
The Book of Chagford • Iain Rice
The Book of Chapel-en-le-Frith • Mike Smith
*The Book of Chittlehamholt with
Warkleigh & Satterleigh* • Richard Lethbridge
The Book of Chittlehampton • Various
The Book of Codford • Romy Wyeth
The Book of Colney Heath • Bryan Lilley
The Book of Constantine • Moore and Trethowan
The Book of Cornwood and Lutton • Compiled by
the People of the Parish

The Book of Crediton • John Heal
The Book of Creech St Michael • June Small
The Book of Crowcombe, Bicknoller and Sampford Brett •
Maurice and Joyce Chidgey
The Book of Crudwell • Tony Pain
The Book of Cullompton • Compiled by the People
of the Parish
The Book of Dawlish • Frank Pearce
*The Book of Dulverton, Brushford,
Bury & Exebridge* • Dulverton and District Civic Society
The Book of Dunster • Hilary Binding
The Book of Easton • Easton Village History Project
The Book of Edale • Gordon Miller
The Ellacombe Book • Sydney R. Langmead
The Book of Exmouth • W.H. Pascoe
The Book of Grampound with Creed • Bane and Oliver
The Book of Gosport • Lesley Burton and
Brian Musselwhite
The Book of Haughley • Howard Stephens
The Book of Hayle • Harry Pascoe
The Book of Hayling Island & Langstone • Peter Rogers
The Book of Helston • Jenkin with Carter
The Book of Hemyock • Clist and Dracott
The Book of Herne Hill • Patricia Jenkyns
The Book of Hethersett • Hethersett Society
Research Group
The Book of High Bickington • Avril Stone
The Book of Honiton • Gerald Gosling
The Book of Ilsington • Dick Wills
The Book of Kingskerswell • Carsewella Local
History Group
The Book of Lamerton • Ann Cole and Friends
Lanner, A Cornish Mining Parish • Sharron
Schwartz and Roger Parker
The Book of Leigh & Bransford • Malcolm Scott
The Second Book of Leigh & Bransford • Malcolm Scott
The Book of Litcham with Lexham & Mileham • Litcham
Historical and Amenity Society
The Book of Llangain • Haydyn Williams
The Book of Loddiswell • Loddiswell Parish History Group
The New Book of Lostwithiel • Barbara Fraser
The Book of Lulworth • Rodney Legg
The Book of Lustleigh • Joe Crowdy
The Book of Lydford • Compiled by Barbara Weeks
The Book of Lyme Regis • Rodney Legg
The Book of Manaton • Compiled by the People
of the Parish

The Book of Markyate • Markyate Local History Society

The Book of Mawnan • Mawnan Local History Group

The Book of Meavy • Pauline Hemery

The Book of Mere • Dr David Longbourne

The Book of Minehead with Alcombe • Binding and Stevens

The Book of Monks Orchard and Eden Park • Ian Muir and Pat Manning

The Book of Morchard Bishop • Jeff Kingaby

The Book of Mylor • Mylor Local History Group

The Book of Narborough • Narborough Local History Society

The Book of Newdigate • John Callcut

The Book of Newtown • Keir Foss

The Book of Nidderdale • Nidderdale Museum Society

The Book of Northlew with Ashbury • Northlew History Group

The Book of North Newton • J.C. and K.C. Robins

The Book of North Tawton • Baker, Hoare and Shields

The Book of Nynehead • Nynehead & District History Society

The Book of Okehampton • Roy and Ursula Radford

The Book of Ottery St Mary • Gerald Gosling and Peter Harris

The Book of Paignton • Frank Pearce

The Book of Penge, Anerley & Crystal Palace • Peter Abbott

The Book of Peter Tavy with Cudlipptown • Peter Tavy Heritage Group

The Book of Pimperne • Jean Coull

The Book of Plymtree • Tony Eames

The Book of Poole • Rodney Legg

The Book of Porlock • Dennis Corner

Postbridge – The Heart of Dartmoor • Reg Bellamy

The Book of Priddy • Albert Thompson

The Book of Princetown • Dr Gardner-Thorpe

The Book of Probus • Alan Kent and Danny Merrifield

The Book of Rattery • By the People of the Parish

The Book of Roadwater, Leighland and Treborough • Clare and Glyn Court

The Book of St Austell • Peter Hancock

The Book of St Day • Joseph Mills and Paul Annear

The Book of St Dennis and Goss Moor • Kenneth Rickard

The Book of St Levan • St Levan Local History Group

The Book of Sampford Courtenay with Honeychurch • Stephanie Pouya

The Book of Sculthorpe • Gary Windeler

The Book of Seaton • Ted Gosling

The Book of Sidmouth • Ted Gosling and Sheila Luxton

The Book of Silverton • Silverton Local History Society

The Book of South Molton • Jonathan Edmunds

The Book of South Stoke with Midford • Edited by Robert Parfitt

South Tawton & South Zeal with Sticklepath • Roy and Ursula Radford

The Book of Sparkwell with Hemerdon & Lee Mill • Pam James

The Book of Staverton • Pete Lavis

The Book of Stithians • Stithians Parish History Group

The Book of Stogumber, Monksilver, Nettlecombe & Elworthy • Maurice and Joyce Chidgey

The Book of South Brent • Greg Wall

The Book of Studland • Rodney Legg

The Book of Swanage • Rodney Legg

The Book of Tavistock • Gerry Woodcock

The Book of Thorley • Sylvia McDonald and Bill Hardy

The Book of Torbay • Frank Pearce

The Book of Truro • Christine Parnell

The Book of Uplyme • Gerald Gosling and Jack Thomas

The Book of Watchet • Compiled by David Banks

The Book of Wendling, Longham and Beeston with Bittering • Stephen Olley

The Book of West Huntspill • By the People of the Parish

The Book of Weston-super-Mare • Sharon Poole

The Book of Whitchurch • Gerry Woodcock

Widecombe-in-the-Moor • Stephen Woods

Widecombe – Uncle Tom Cobley & All • Stephen Woods

The Book of Williton • Michael Williams

The Book of Wincanton • Rodney Legg

The Book of Winscombe • Margaret Tucker

The Book of Witheridge • Peter and Freda Tout and John Usmar

The Book of Withycombe • Chris Boyles

Woodbury: The Twentieth Century Revisited • Roger Stokes

The Book of Woolmer Green • Compiled by the People of the Parish

The Book of Yetminster • Shelagh Hill

For details of any of the above titles or if you are interested in writing your own history, please contact: Commissioning Editor, Community Histories, Halsgrove House, Lower Moor Way, Tiverton, Devon EX16 6SS, England; email: katyc@halsgrove.com